How Delicate
These Arches

Also by David Feela

Thought Experiments
(Southwest Poets' Series chapbook winner),
Maverick Press, 1998

The Home Atlas
WordTech Editions, 2009

How Delicate These Arches

Footnotes from the Four Corners

by David Feela

Raven's Eye Press
Durango, Colorado

Raven's Eye Press
Durango, Colorado
www.ravenseyepress.com

Feela, David.
  How Delicate These Arches: Footnotes from the Four
Corners/David Feela
    p. cm.

1. Nature
2. Southwest
3. Humor
I. Title

ISBN: 978-0-9816584-8-3
LCCN: 2011934003

Cover & interior design by Lindsay J. Nyquist, *elle jay design*
Initial cover concept, Pam Smith

Printed in the United States of America
1 3 5 7 9 10 8 6 4 2

Dedication

4 Pam

4 Pam

4 Pam

4 Pam

companion in word & deed

Acknowledgments

For over a decade many fine writers and editors have helped sponsor me in the publishing world, where much of this work first appeared, some of it in a slightly different form.

Many thanks to the following:

Betsy and Ed Marston of the *High Country News's* "Writers on the Range"

Ken Wright, Phil Lauro, Pete Prendergast, and Jan Nesset of *The Durango Herald's Inside/Outside Southwest Magazine*

Gail Binkly and Wendy Mimiaga of the *Four Corners Free Press*

Sue O'Brien of *The Denver Post's* "Colorado Voices"

Some of this writing has appeared in the following publications and anthologies:

Utne, Reader, November/December, 2010
Small Farmer's Journal, Spring, 2008

Tree Magic, SunShine Press Publication, c2005
Powerful Classroom Stories from Accomplished Teachers,
    Corwin Press, c2004
Mountain Gazette, #84, 2002
Living in the Runaway West, *High Country News,* c2000
No Shit! There I Was...At Last!, ICS Books, c1997
Sport Literate, #8, 1997
Potomac Review, Summer, 1996
The San Juan Almanac, 1996

Table of Contents

The Road, Again

Preface

I can only imagine how unconnected so many travelers must feel passing through the desert Southwest. Their instinctual GPS steers them clear of any complex community encounters and heads them straight toward Utah's Canyonlands, or parks them at the Four Corners Monument to take a photograph with their loved ones standing on the only point in the continental US where four state borders converge, then nudges them on toward that great dip in the road, the Grand Canyon.

If you follow this itinerary, you may see the sights but sadly, you'll miss the experience. This book isn't a destination guide. It's like an outfitter's guarantee to his customers that you paid good money for more than just a tour.

All of the events rendered here are real, micro-essays that have been brewing for over a decade. Or, to frame the idea more soberly, they are snapshots from where I live, verbal polaroids that will develop before your eyes, revealing what the legend on any map can not identify. All of these essays have appeared for public viewing in regional sources, such as the recently deceased Inside/Outside Southwest magazine, The Denver Post, The High Country News's syndicated column, "Writers on the Range," and the Four Corners Free Press. Some have been anthologized in regional and national publications. Reading is, after all, the great compass by which we orient ourselves. You may discover that no matter where you're from, our experiences converge like an intersection.

The narrative contained within compiles a kind of scrapbook, an insider's guide to what's not visible from the highway. In the simplest terms, this is reportage from my corner of the American West. In a broader stroke, these essays focus on the crossroads where unpredictable people and public policy, public lands and semi-wildlife merge. It begins in my driveway and wanders into a vast landscape colored by so much more than mere sunrises and sunsets, rocks and ruins.

Thirty years ago I never planned on staying. Now I can't imagine ever leaving. And all the years between continue to sculpt one more delicate sandstone arch, as improbable as it is beautiful.

section one

The Longest Driveway

CHAPTER ONE

The watermelon whisperer

For decades, when the summer melons rolled into the produce aisles, my mouth would water and I'd buy the biggest one. Unfortunately, not every watermelon is endowed with the same inalienable perfection, and I have carted home quite a few duds. Until I met Margaret in the produce aisle.

If this sounds like a soap opera, it's because I had humongous twin melons strapped into the child seat of my grocery cart. That's when I saw Margaret. We slowed our carts, paused, and exchanged warm greetings. She had a single watermelon about the size of a soccer ball, a dark and glossy green one that reminds me of unripe fruit.

"Are you going to buy both of those?" Margaret asked me.

"And eat them too," I replied, flashing her a wide watermelon grin. "I hope they're as good as they look."

"Well, really, David, they don't look all that good."

I was shocked. Normally people who work at the library are quiet types who respect other people's choices and try to help out when their advice is sought. Margaret had been this and more during the 20 years I had known her, but I'd never tried to talk with her over the business end of a watermelon.

Then I remembered who I was talking to: It was Margaret – kind, sweet Margaret – the lady who helped me through graduate school by locating the stacks of resources, the Margaret who always says something nice about my latest column, the Margaret who has worked in our library since the library in Alexandria was burned by the Romans. That Margaret. I could trust Margaret.

"Honestly," I stammered, "I've don't have a clue about choosing watermelons."

Margaret looked at me with those sympathetic but all-knowing reference librarian eyes, picked up the melon from her cart, and held it as if it were a puppy. Then she instructed me in the art of reading watermelons.

First, look for the sugar spot on the bottom, yellowish or white, where the belly of the melon rested on the ground. The sugar spot says it will be sweet.

Second, the coloring should be a glossy green, not pale or sickly yellow.

Finally, hold the melon up and thump it quickly as you would a drum; the vibration should radiate through the entire melon.

I stared at the pathetic twins in my cart: No sugar spots, both of them pale and resonating like bricks. Margaret sensed a dark shadow of realization crossing my face.

"Don't worry, David, it's very easy – try again." Then

she waved and moved on down the aisle.

To be literate and educated is never enough. The watermelons I loved were suddenly new. With my new knowledge, I rushed toward the palate at the front of the store where they were confined in bins, waiting to be chosen. One of them – just one – would be perfect and waiting for me.

Of course, Margaret must have known what she'd done. Her eyes twinkled as she walked away, as if to say a seed has been planted. And planting seeds is so much easier than juggling watermelons.

CHAPTER TWO

My favorite mountain

A national park with sunset views of a comatose mountain. A self-guided nature tour through the sage and rabbit brush providing the desert Southwest's version of aroma-therapy for the camper's soul. And as a bonus, because the piñons in the park are mostly without needles, dried up or dead, the unfiltered sound of irrigation water rushing down an open ditch.

As darkness descends, a semi-qualified and mostly compassionate park official joins you beside the campfire to narrate the legend of that old Sleeping Ute warrior stretched out against the western horizon, a tale of how one day he may rise from his long nap to stomp any and all unappreciative campers right into the ground. A story guaranteed to quiet your children. Yes, My Backyard National Park would be the perfect place to cool your wheels or rest your heels. Just follow the cardboard signs stapled beside the garage sale notices on posts all over town. You can't miss it.

You see, the Sleeping Ute Mountain calms me, since every other officially mountainous national park is overused, understaffed, and poorly funded, which is why I am offering to designate my 11 acres of mostly sagebrush as a national park. The view from my backyard is just too beautiful to keep to myself.

Not many mountains seem to float in the high desert air as perfectly as this one. Though its entire corpus is located within the boundaries of the Ute reservation, it hovers out there as a peaceful reminder that our cultural differences are a part of this American landscape.

It's also geological poetry, because I can't help thinking of T.S. Eliot's memorable lines at sunset:

> *Let us go then, you and I,*
> *When the evening is spread out against the sky*
> *Like a patient etherised upon a table.*

I know the whole idea of designating and running my own national park seems a bit out there, but the way I see it, something needs to be done to foster an appreciation of one of the Southwest's most understated and unappreciated mountains.

Imagine the view from Mesa Verde National Park as a bus with 50 French explorers unloads beside the Cliff Palace ruins. The ranger in charge points them to the overlook for pictures and then with a gesture in my direction, "And over there is that guy's sagebrush kingdom where you can open a beer and hear how the Sleeping Ute has terrorized residents for centuries."

Chapter Three

An ounce of oil, a pound of humility

My first chainsaw arrived 25 years ago, a Christmas gift from my mother-in-law. It was a brand new Homelite with a 12 inch bar. It looked like a gas-powered carving knife, but I proclaimed my thanks and quietly promised my wife I wouldn't start it up when the turkey came out of the oven. The chainsaw lasted one winter, relegated mostly to gnawing at kindling. I'll admit there were times it worked better than my two-man saw when the man on the other side turned out to be a 110 pound woman, but the carburetor went bad and the saw choked. I sold it at a garage sale to a neighbor who claimed he knew how to fix those things. I never saw or heard that saw again, and come to think of it, I don't have much recollection of the neighbor either.

I waited 10 years to buy my next chainsaw. It's not that I couldn't afford one. No, those were my purist years, when the act of cutting trees served as ritual, a pilgrimage to the woods to worship the living while salvaging the fallen or the standing dead. My double-bladed axe became an instrument of atonement, its edges filed and honed to perfection, its handle flexed to exert all the power I could wield from within. I relished going out to split logs in the sub-zero mornings. Aldo Leopold wrote, "If one has cut, split, hauled, and piled his own good oak...he will remember much about where the heat comes from."

Maybe I overheated, because the second chainsaw I owned was electric. It seemed a perfect solution to the dirty, noisy, unreliable antics of gas-powered wood cutting. I would simply haul the trees like a logger, then slice them up like butter in the comfort of my own backyard. Pretty slick, I thought, but after a few seasons of tangled, nicked, and sliced extension cords, a plug that worked loose every 10 minutes unless I duct-taped it to the saw, blown circuit breakers, and a burned out wall socket, I decided no serious sawyer had any business cutting wood tethered to the Co-op's power grid.

Eventually I got rid of wood burning stoves altogether and by association, the chore of cutting wood. My energy went into lawn mowing, weed whacking, and dust busting. My life would have remained chainsaw-free if not for the piñon beetle.

Something had to be done with my miniature forest of dead piñon trees. Solution? Buy a reconditioned chainsaw. Since I wasn't cutting wood to heat a house, I reasoned I didn't need state-of-the-art machinery. A serviceable saw with a 90 day guarantee seemed perfect to me. I could cut a lot of piñon in 90 days. So what if the chainsaw sold without an instruction manual, spec sheet, or any sort of documentation. I could figure it out, couldn't I? How complicated could a chainsaw be?

I carried the saw home, gassed up, and headed toward the piñons. I still owned the axe but – how shall I say this? – it had lost its edge, deteriorated, seemed heavier than it used to be.

The first tree came down in all of 50 seconds. I stood beside the stump and counted over 50 growth rings etched in its trunk. In my hand the chainsaw purred. I moved to the second tree, considerably smaller, but just as brown and brittle as the first. With the throttle pushed flat, the saw roared to life, and the chain spit sawdust until the ground turned white. Before I finished number three, a little stutter stirred in the machine, while heat waves shimmered beside the engine vent. By number four, the chainsaw gasped; the fifth made the chainsaw ill, and halfway through number six, it died. I pulled the starter cord: Flooded. I yanked again, and again, and well... let's just say even I sputtered.

My toolbox at hand, I sat in the shade of a dead pinion and removed the plastic guard so I could manipulate the sprocket with my fingers. It must be sticking, I thought, and when I touched the metal spool the pain flashed to my head, ran back down the length of my spine, and out my mouth – a yelp that sounded like a dog. The metal had been tempered blue with heat, while the skin on my fingers (and probably my face) blanched white.

At the shop I explained how the chainsaw ran fine when it was cool, but as it heated up it sputtered, stuttered, and stopped. I thought something might be binding and pointed with my bandaged finger.

The repairman glanced toward the sprocket, then unscrewed the gas cap and poured the remaining fuel into a glass

Mason jar. He held the jar up to the light like it was a specimen, then set it on the counter between us before he looked at me.

"What kind of oil mixture are you using?" he asked.

"One of those little bottles, I don't know exactly how much without looking at it, in a gallon of gas. Two cycle oil, right? No wait..." and then it dawned on me. That's the mixture I used in my weed trimmer; I'd filled the chainsaw with straight gasoline.

"You know," the repairman said in a soft voice, "when there's no dipstick on an engine the oil has got to go into the gas."

I knew what a dipstick was, and now I knew how a dipstick felt.

I stared at the counter, at the Mason jar, as if the amber liquid could predict the chainsaw's future. "Did I ruin the engine?" was all I could think to ask.

Without a word the repairman took the chainsaw into a back room and a few minutes later I heard it start. It coughed, but then it ran, and he let it run for a couple minutes, accelerating, dropping back to idle, racing the engine again. Then he shut it off and set it on the counter between us.

For the first time in 10 minutes I looked into his eyes. "Thank you for being smarter than the operator." He glanced back down toward the counter, pointing at the gas cap on the chainsaw.

"You see that little picture of the gas pump?" he asked.

"Yes, I've seen those at gas stations before."

"Well, that tiny icon of a drop next to the gas pump is supposed to stand for oil. They both go in this hole, together."

I smiled. He looked up and we both laughed. "How

much do I owe you?" I asked, reaching for my wallet.

He told me there was no charge, so I bought a tiny bottle 2 cycle oil, knowing it wasn't enough to show my appreciation. But as I walked out the door I could see him smiling and shaking his head. I knew he now had one of those stories to tell, the kind that cause people to raise their eyebrows and laugh out loud. The kind of story that's priceless.

CHAPTER FOUR

The fuel on the hill

I owned a wood stove once. Actually, the stove owned me. It consumed every stick I fed into it, then it stared longingly out toward the trees.

We were young, deciding to change our little three-room house over to wood heat, green as the trees we foolishly hauled in from the country. It didn't take long to learn that where there's smoke there's not necessarily fire.

More often, though, as our experiences smoldered, I grew less enchanted with my wood burning chores, staying in bed as long as I could, buried to our noses under a mountain of blankets and quilts. When I finally couldn't avoid the inevitable, I'd slip into my union suit, intending to lay a rip-roaring fire in record time and rush back to the coals of my dreams while the house warmed itself to a more hospitable temperature. From the tropical island of our bed, we'd listen to the clanking racket cold iron makes when it's startled to life by a fitful passion of flame.

Of course, things rarely go according to plan, especially when dealing with wood stoves. More often than not the ash tin brims and needs emptying. Then the can where the ashes get emptied brims too, and it needs to be emptied. Or the convenient stack of wood I thought I'd left just outside the door gets hauled away by the wood elves, prompting a major expedition through the snow to the woodshed.

You'd think we were cold all the time, but no, our place was the only house in our neighborhood where the doors stayed propped open on the coldest nights. Even the dog crawled outside for relief, preferring the temperate glow of the moon and stars.

I can't forget the fire behind the chimney wall that provided us with one more reason to reconsider our roles as primitive fire-builders. Why I climbed to the roof to smother the chimney I'll never understand, because instead of taking away the fire's oxygen and quickly extinguishing our danger, I prompted the entire house to fill with smoke. My wife roused a neighbor and together they choked and gasped while pulling down the chimney wall with a couple crowbars. They may have saved the house, but I knew for the first time that evening that the wood stove was on its way out.

We hauled wood for another year, learning to count our months by the cord. Eventually we had wood delivered, but we were never delivered from the labor of wood. I hauled my wood twice, as stove length pieces and as ash. Once each month on Sunday morning I religiously scraped our chimney clean. I singed my eyebrows, we both burned holes in our favorite sleeves. We scrubbed and repainted the ceilings each spring, trying to restore them to their former purity. Sharpening blades, filing saw teeth, replacing axe handles, pulling, sputtering, and choking the daylights out of more than a few chainsaws, we came to dread even the philosophical sound a tree makes when it falls in the woods. With our luck, it always landed directly on another beautiful autumn weekend.

Aldo Leopold wrote that splitting good oak gives one "a wealth of detail denied to those who spend the weekend in town astride a radiator" and I know he's right. Judging by the cloud of wood smoke that hovers over my little town, there are still a lot of wood-burners out there. When the air gets too thick to breathe, maybe we can burn it.

Our wood stove moved in with a mountain man who appreciates its appetite for attention. I've been wooed by a propane model fireplace where a chorus line of tiny blue flames dances whenever the thermostat says it's time. We like the new stove's simplicity, the opportunity to put another metaphoric log on the fire by twisting a dial. Who knows what will become of the time we've saved. Maybe I'll write a book. And if that doesn't work out, I'll have the effort to pass along as kindling.

CHAPTER FIVE

They call it a courtesy

Recently, a Colorado Highway Patrol trooper pulled me over, or maybe it would be more precise to say, I made room for him on the shoulder. I had driven barely a quarter mile from my house at a breakneck speed of 25 mph, preparing to travel on Highway 491. I knew immediately what I had done: I'd failed to come to a complete stop at the sign before entering the highway, but rather than meditate on my crime, I recalled an old joke about a man who upon hearing that most accidents occur within 25 miles of home decided to move.

I'm not saying the trooper was wrong. I'm not even saying I had an excuse, though my brain worked very quickly trying to think one up. Rather, I was a victim of bad timing, a cosmic offense for which the universe is routinely punishing me. The officer must have blessed his perfect day – I was waiting on the shoulder even before he got around to turning his lights on.

Nobody wants to hear my explanation, though the officer involved was obliged to listen to it, because he foolishly asked the question, "Do you know why I pulled you over?" Since he had to listen, so do you.

My county road climbs an embankment to meet the highway, leaving me on an incline where the stop sign has been planted. When the road is covered by snow or ice, my wheels spin and the car slides backward if I come to a full stop. In bad weather I usually creep up the slope and past the stop sign, pulling immediately to the shoulder, and from that position I wait for my best chance at merging with highway traffic.

On this particular day the snow and ice had thawed, but my habit of creeping past the stop sign stayed firm. That's the way it goes with habits, and why people habitually call them by that name. I offered my license, registration, and proof of insurance. I stayed calm. I remained polite. After instructing me to stay in my car, he went back to his.

I sat like an accused man for over 20 minutes. No doubt he called my numbers in, waiting for a report on my criminal history. I kept glancing at the mirror, trying to figure out what could be taking so long. I had no outstanding warrants, no expired or improperly executed paperwork. I was an unwanted man.

I'd rather have been talking with the trooper about the drivers that use the shoulder to recklessly pass me while I'm waiting to make a left turn off the same highway. It happens a couple times a week, sometimes more. A vehicle blows past me on the shoulder at sixty-five miles an hour, a gust of wind that rocks my little car and feeds images of twisted pretzels through my brain. But the officer was busy doing his paperwork. I had to wait.

If you, too, are waiting, perhaps for this paragraph to end, may I take a moment of your time to ask you, please, to use a little caution and patience. Slow down – even come to a full stop if you have to. Let the poor fellow in front of you make his left turn. Don't use the shoulder to pass a vehicle that's signaling a left turn. I know. I used to do that too.

In the end, I received a courtesy warning, the kind of citation that says, We noticed you driving a little dangerously but we're going to give you a second chance. I was relieved. All the way into town I vowed to stop completely at each and every stop sign. And I did. And I do. Courtesy warnings have that effect: They reward you for your patience.

You can go now.

CHAPTER SIX

Desperados

Legends of outlaws hiding out during the "Good Old Days" have made the Southwest especially attractive to tourists. Butch Cassidy and his buddy named Sundance, the Dalton Gang, even Billy the Kid holed up in some of the most out-of-the-way places because they just didn't want to go home again.

When my wife's parents showed up for an entire month, I didn't want to go home either. They wore smiles instead of guns but because I inherited them as relatives when I made off with their daughter's heart, the law was on their side: They were the in-laws and I did the time.

When they arrived they quickly transformed the guestroom into a cave by closing the curtains and leaving the jaws of their suitcases opened like bear traps on the floor. All month they got up each morning separately, about an hour apart. The first one snorted and sneezed, then squinted into the daylight expecting to be served a hot meal as he plopped down beside the table.

Here was the leader of the gang, my father-in-law, a man who never learned to cook but claims to know everything about it. He needs a hearing aid, though he'll never admit that. My wife Pam will ask if he wants eggs or pancakes and he'll say, yeah, his legs got a little cold last night. She'll ask again if he wants two eggs and he'll say, yeah, both legs. So she'll pull two eggs out of the refrigerator and crack them on the edge of the skillet before he notices and asks her why we're having eggs again.

He'll chew his own food, but he won't put creamer in his own coffee, he won't put his dirty dishes in the sink. He's not much of a conversationalist while he eats, though he will grunt at questions or comments that interest him. When he's finished, he'll push his chair back from the table and wait, doing his part in helping us clear the table by moving his stomach out of the way.

My mother-in-law is the brain of the outfit. She appears for breakfast around noon. Her eyes won't focus because she refuses to wear her glasses, but her ears work like a bat's. She can hear what I'm thinking when I'm at the other end of the house, and she'll choose the most inconvenient moment to ask for help – like when I'm at the other end of the house. By mid-afternoon they're both slouched like exhausted gunslingers in opposite corners of the living room. How they could be exhausted by the effort it takes to digest food is a matter science has yet to answer.

At first I thought it seemed like a good idea to put both of them in the car and take them for a little outing: Some fresh air, a new scene. But just loading them into the car was enough to convince me that half the world's mistakes are born of good intentions. Pam settled the argument over who would sit next to me in the front seat by ordering both of them to shut up and sit in the back – she's not really been herself this autumn. Just listen to what she said: She told her own parents to shut up.

We stopped at a restaurant for lunch. I made sure it was far enough out of town so the customers would think we're just travelers on the way to some other place. The waitress was pleasant enough, laughing good-naturedly at the string of come-on lines my father-in-law tries on every waitress he has ever encountered. She deserves a good tip just for listening to him while Pam situates her mother and tries to read to her what the menu has to offer.

My mother-in-law likes going out to eat. She likes to tell us what she likes and what she doesn't like. She even tells us what her husband likes, and especially what doesn't agree with him anymore. I can see the waitress getting anxious, that other tables are filling up. If I send her away – which would be the humane thing to do – she'll probably avoid our table for a long time, but if I force my in-laws to order right now, I'll have to listen to their complaints about the food all the way back to Cortez.

Then I notice the buffet in the corner: One of those all-you-can-eat feeding troughs where everybody goes away happy. Before anyone can say "Oink" I've ordered four buffet tickets and quickly added that the treat is on us. It only occurs to me after the waitress has smiled and left us that Pam will be the one nudging her mother through the line by her elbow, her mother's nose leaving a streak along the steamy glass, asking what's that, and what's that? while a crowd of hungry truckers will be right up against her bumper. And my father-in-law, of course, will expect me to refill his plate "while I'm up."

Even when he's not eating, my father-in-law fails miserably at conversation. If he is a social animal, then he's the type that circles its prey and talks it to death, the air around him bloodied with the blather of his voice. He uses the phrase "by the way..." to give himself permission for bringing in any unrelated topic without having to make transitional sense. And because his hearing is so bad, he shouts. When my mother-in-law corrects what he misunderstood, they always sound like they're arguing, because she shouts back at him until he finally says "oh" and then the blather starts again.

It doesn't take long before we glaze over and give up trying to say anything meaningful, for it doesn't matter what we say, he'll say he knows better, or he'll say, "yeah, you see, I taught you something."

By the way, have you ever noticed how much gravel it takes to fill a muddy hole in the driveway? Some unnatural force keeps pushing whatever you dump into it toward the center of the earth so it appears as if you've done nothing. This is a lot like all the attention we've been heaping on these guests since they arrived: For some unnatural reason they have yet to thank us for anything that has happened in nearly a month. I'd like to pretend that my elderly in-laws are similar to children and that time has simply reversed our roles. But I know the very idea that aging people turn into children again is at best a platitude; at worst, it's an outright lie.

The problem with comparing my in-laws to children is that we can tell them to go to their room but they won't go. So we go to ours and my father-in-law follows us, so Pam goes to the bathroom and shuts the door to sit on the toilet for five minutes of peace, but five minutes later he's opening the bathroom door to tell her how to prune her fruit trees. Of course, she has been constipated for a week. She demands he at least respect her privacy; he counters by reminding her that he changed her diapers. It may not be the kind of movement she was hoping for this month, but slamming the door is the only relief she's going to get.

CHAPTER SEVEN

Faint Glory

*"It's not so difficult to feel like a fool when you
actually behave like one."*
—from *Faintly Coherent*
(a book I still intend to write)

My mother marched the three of us into the doctor's office and ordered us to behave. After she'd filled out a stack of papers, the doctor called us in for our immunizations. At the time, I didn't know what a shot was and I don't think I would have liked the sound of it, but luckily my mother used the bigger word, Immunizations. When the doctor asked which of us would volunteer to be first, I stepped forward and declared, "I'm not afraid."

He swabbed my arm with alcohol and stuck the needle into me. When he finished I turned toward my quivering siblings and proudly announced, "There, that didn't hurt" then promptly passed out. Supposedly the screams from my terrorized brother and sister were enough to shut that office down for ten full minutes while my mother shushed them and shoed them out the door. I can't account for the details of this melee, because those minutes were taken from me, melded into a blur I now refer to as down time.

Since then I have passed out dozens of times. Each occasion embarrasses me, but none more so than the time I held my cat for his distemper shot and I keeled over backward, smashing my skull on the doorknob. The cat went flying, and after the vet put his eyes back into his head, he ministered to me as I returned to the conscious world. "Where am I?" I reportedly asked. "You are on the floor," replied the vet, "and your cat ran out the door." It could be that my state of disorientation transported me for an instant into a Dr. Seuss book.

Once in the 1970s during a swine flu scare, I went over onto a mattress that had been arranged on the armory floor to collect the falling bodies. Not only did I land on the mattress, but I found myself positioned between the softest parts of a very buxom woman who had sprawled there before me. The encounter would have been even more embarrassing than my usual faint except that the woman was more out of it than I was, and I managed to regain my stature before she could regain her composure.

These days I disclose to medical professionals my likelihood to faint, or, as one doctor put it, to engage my hyperactive vagal nerve. Supposedly, the vagal response is a leftover instinct from primitive times, when fear sent a high-powered jolt of adrenaline through the body so the just-getting-on-their-feet homo sapiens could outrun, say, a tiger looking for some not-so-fast food. When the adrenalin kicks in, blood pressure drops, which prompts me to drop. Supposedly, wrestling the tiger would put the wasted adrenalin to work and save me the embarrassment of fainting, but I'm not sure which would be worse.

Nowadays, I try to avoid situations where I might conk out, like volunteering to be a blood donor or running down to the supermarket to pick up a dozen eggs and a shingles vaccination, but I know the possibility will remain with me for the rest of my life. It may even prove to be my death. Last year I flatlined after a colonoscopy procedure, and a few months ago a toothache knocked me out cold on my own bathroom floor at three in the morning. I have scars on my face to prove it.

I know I'm not the only person suffering with this condition. I should form a group, Vagals Anonymous, so others can share their experiences and come to terms with the fear and shame of slipping uncontrollably into the unconscious world. I'm afraid, however, that at the first meeting I'd stand up, state my name, and immediately pass out.

CHAPTER EIGHT

How to be a doctor without leaving your recliner

It was cold outside and I wasn't feeling so great, but I didn't know how to describe what was wrong. I should have gone to the doctor, but with gas prices out of control, my medical co-pay doing the double-whammy along with my monthly insurance premiums, and my prescription drug costs replacing some of the food I normally put in my mouth, I decided on a more frugal means of discovering what troubled me.

I turned on the television.

It's difficult to believe all the debate in Washington about health care reform for the last decade has accomplished nothing, at least nothing more than opening the door for drug companies to bring their products to prime time. If you watch television, it becomes increasingly obvious that the commercialization of illness has become the public's first line of defense in treating our ailments. I wondered if a television consultation would work for me, so instead of sitting in a waiting room I sat down in my recliner and aimed the remote control. Pushing the buttons, my fingers felt stiff and achy. Definitely the onset of an illness, but which one?

The first commercial I watched discussed achy legs, not fingers. As I got to thinking about it, my legs weren't doing so well either. The ad-man called it Restless Leg Syndrome, or RLS (a handy little acronym to help me remember what my problem might be). I wrote it down on the notepad beside my chair along with the prescribed medication and continued to surf the networks.

Next I heard about BPH, which turned out to be another way of saying Benign Prostatic Hyperplasia, more commonly referred to as an uncontrollable urge to pee. Average looking people on the television were gasping and dashing toward a bathroom. The ad said, "If you're experiencing symptoms such as...frequently waking up at night to go, you might have a potential problem." I copied the number on my notepad. Their offer for a one week free trial sounded tempting. I haven't had a full night's sleeping without getting up to pee since I turned 45.

Eventually the "little purple pill" appeared, and I listened closely to hear if I was suffering from something it might resolve. A fatherly looking actor went around the house telling his studio children to finish up whatever they were doing and then he produced a sour expression. This must be what actors do, I thought, because I recognized the look, even had the bitter taste of it in my mouth as he spoke to a Hollywood doctor about the risk of his esophagus burning up. I wasn't sure if stomach acid could make my fingers and legs ache, but I jotted it down, just in case I decided to take the salsa out of the refrigerator for lunch.

I breezed through a few smaller ads about common aches and pains, ending in sales pitches for over-the-counter relief. But my achiness felt more serious, something that "take two aspirins and call me in the morning" wouldn't cure.

When I saw the handsome, happy couple focusing all their attention on each other, I had to stop and watch. It turned out that his problem was ED (as in EEEEE DEEEE), and I don't mean it as an acronym for the word Education, although I learned quite a bit just listening to the list of side-effects. I certainly wasn't experiencing any of that, but in the back of my head I kept wondering if a stiffness in the limbs was how it all started. She looked pleased that he'd done something about his problem, and her smile certainly deserved an Emmy.

These medical dilemmas on television were not running out of patients, but I was. Diseased incarnations fashioned as artery blockages, irritable bowels, high cholesterol, migraines, skin rashes, hair loss, and diarrhea made their way into my living room and offered themselves to me like voodoo dolls. When I turned the television off, I felt worse than when I sat down, because every medical scenario had been marketed to appeal to me, to encourage me to consult a doctor, armed with a crib sheet full of symptoms and a shopping list of drugs.

When the doctor finally entered the examining room all he'd have to say would be, "Which commercial did you watch?" I'd consult my notes, give the correct channel, time, and date, and we could review my diagnosis on a Tivo, share some small talk while I'm waiting for my prescription. Yes, I'd say, I've been studying medicine now for most of the fall season.

My mother would be proud. She always wanted me to be a doctor.

CHAPTER NINE

I've got the power

It isn't like one of those holiday scenes with snow swirling, caught inside a vigorously shaken globe of winter wonder. It's only a glass cylinder about the size of a three-pound coffee can, attached to my telephone post. A silver disc spins inside it. Vaguely resembling a CD player, it's known in the utilities business as an electric meter. It measures my indulgences.

A long time ago, an employee from the electric company used to stop by to read its numbers. Eventually, customers were asked to read their own numbers. Then about ten years ago the electric company replaced my old meter, and when I looked out my window after dark, a tiny red light winked back at me from under the glass, steady as an omnipotent eye. Now my meter reads itself.

Benjamin Franklin's experiment with electricity involved a kite, a key, and a lightning bolt. Frankly, he was taking far more chances than I would take. My experiment required only a flashlight and a steady hand. It involved going outside one night to watch the meter spin.

I'll admit I didn't come to any earth-shattering conclusion other than noticing how each revolution was costing me money, so I went back to the house and turned on every big name-brand appliance I owned, then plugged in every Christmas light. In other words, I cranked it up a bit, just to see how much faster the meter moved. It whirled.

Next, I went back into the house and shut everything off. I assumed the meter would slow down, which it did, but I was surprised to see that it never stopped. I returned inside and unplugged each and every cord from its wall socket. It continued to spin. Something – maybe just the pull of the moon – wouldn't allow my meter to quit. Who knows? It's even possible that, like a hamster in its cage, I had been expending enough energy running back and forth to the house to keep the wheel turning.

Since this experience, my first consumer-based experiment, I've located more than a few permanent electrical leaks in my home, most of them approved of or even sponsored by corporate manufacturers and, more than likely, the electric company.

It's shocking to see how many electrical devices absorb a continuous flow of electricity just to keep in touch. Once they're plugged in, they beep, flash their little lights, wobble and whir, making all the sounds to let me know they're pleased. In other words, they are manufactured like parasites, to attach themselves to the grid and suck it dry until the device overeats, or the power company goes belly-up, whichever comes first.

Granted, most of these devices require only a trickle of juice to keep, say, that tiny red LCD light on the TV, DVD player, or surge protector glowing, or the numerals on yet another digital clock crisp enough to read. I counted 14 clocks in my house, which helped me decide that it's time for my family to start paying attention to how much electricity we use. The silver disc spins silently, which is probably best, because if it generated a high-pitched whine the faster it spun, I'd have all the neighborhood dogs in my yard, while the entire population of cities like Phoenix or Las Vegas would have their entire populations running for their Civil Defense shelters.

The best answer still comes from the prospect of generating one's own electricity through solar power or any of the alternatives bandied about, such as tapping underground heat or wind. All of the technology has been around for decades, but some people must still believe it's a tree-hugger's dream. I mean, I thought America would be mass-producing fuel-efficient cars right after Nixon lowered the national speed limit to 55 mph.

What I need at my house is a static electrician, someone who can wire the carpeting in my living room and hallway so that the electrical discharge I'm constantly firing off into the unknown can be harnessed. Maybe if I'm lucky, and if I drag my feet the way the government is doing, just maybe I can generate enough electricity during the next cold spell to sell my surplus power back to the electric company.

CHAPTER TEN

The trailers of Montezuma County

It's like a soap-opera romance, this ongoing affection of mine for the old style single or double-wide mobile homes, more commonly known as trailers.

To me their appeal is strongest when I'm driving a gravel county road, and out in a field I see one, perched like an alien spacecraft on a few open acres. Or, I'm turning into the shaded niches of a well-worn trailer park, and it's there, like a time machine, made of corrugated tin and glass. Sometimes it's been repainted, and never the bland manufacturer's color from 30 years ago, but a fresh swath of purple, or yellow, or even turquoise and pink.

I should know: I've been parked since 1986 in a 1972 double-wide. I don't know if it was new when it arrived on the property. It has no wheels, but when I have to climb into the crawl space beneath the mobile home, I can see where wheels would have been mounted. There's not much security down there, knowing that tornados have a sweet tooth for mobile homes. They twist trailers and then spit them out again, but it's still a strange thought: A home could roll in like a tumbleweed and then roll back out again.

My unit is also old enough to probably be illegal, manufactured during the era of pressed board flooring and thin galvanized metal roofing. I've done the mobile home roofover (similar to a middle-aged male combover) and I flush my toilet with caution, realizing that a flood could turn my flooring into waffle wood. Luckily, I live in a generous county that essentially believes, If you can drag it here, we can put up with it, which is why the hardier of these trailers should be preserved, designated as historic local treasures, of no lesser magnitude than those infamous bridges from that county in the Midwest.

The mobile home's survival offers us a reminder of a time when a family's housing ambitions were scaled back to, say, reality. No median sales price hovering around $200,000. No floor space with enough square footage to hold a line dance for a football team. Mobile homes are proof that people could actually live with less, and did. I do now, and its constraint makes certain I continue to do so.

Many others are still living that way, which is why I always slow down to admire these domestic time capsules. The vintage trailer is a covered bridge of sorts, spanning two banks: One side rooted with working people who could at one time own their own homes, and on the other side the current real estate market, where a lifetime of slowly diminishing mortgage debt is the glimmer at the end of tunnel. I know some people consider yesterday's trailers trash when compared to today's modular, custom, set-on-a-slab, instant triple-wide castles. It is fair to say that a trailer does not have the investment potential of a ranchette with a massively imposing entrance gate. Maybe so, but I'd rather spend my days renovating the past than making payments on someone else's future.

I'll admit that much of a trailer's styling, especially during the '60s and '70s, was a little too boxy, but it's tough to argue with a classic advertising slogan, Home is where you park it. For me, the idea of being self-contained has never lost its appeal.

Housing needs are basic for all people, but available housing has taken a nasty turn away from anything approaching basic. In a nearby town, for example, 15 homeowners in the Riverview Trailer Park were evicted to make way for a 39-unit condominium development, some units starting at a lofty $250,000. Such practices happen all across the West each time an economic boom in real estate sends trailer homeowners scurrying for cover. For our own protection as locals, before the next real estate bubble pops, we'd better all be wearing condos, the only safe housing available.

Where's a romantically inclined professional photographer when you need one? Maybe a lanky Clint Eastwood type, someone with an eye to show us the implicit beauty in an antiquated hallway without wheels. And even if the trailers look a little shabby by current standards, they embody a fiscal fantasy we're in danger of forgetting. They stand for autonomy, at least as long as they're allowed to stand.

CHAPTER ELEVEN

The gift of the magpie

In 1906 O'Henry published a short story titled "The Gift of the Magi" about a couple that scrimped and saved to buy each other the perfect Christmas gift. The story's end has a twist, because the woman cuts and sells her hair to buy a fob chain for her love's pocket watch. Unknown to the wife, the husband sells his prized watch to buy a set of combs for her long beautiful hair. It's really a story about love and the awkwardness that flourishes when our desire to surprise each other overwhelms the need to communicate. It's also important to understand that at the turn of the twentieth century when this story supposedly took place, standard retail exchange and return policies did not exist, with or without a receipt.

I have a similar story to tell that takes place in the Southwest, and while it's still about love, it lacks the innocence of O'Henry's classic tale. Pam bought me a special gift: A small writing desk that would fit in our living room near the propane stove. I own two other desks, situated in my study, but in the winter it gets cold at that end of the house. She wanted to buy me this gift because I love words and writing is close to my heart.

Unlike the woman in the story, she told me what she intended to buy, even going so far as to show me on the Internet some desks that were priced within our budget. Which desk did I prefer? she wanted to know. I looked over her shoulder and nodded, but in the end I said, No, thank you very much, I could get along just fine with the desks in the writing room that never got above 62 degrees. Good writing is born of suffering, I said. She sighed.

I wanted to replace a cashmere sweater, the one she bought from a local thrift store a few months before Christmas. She loved it, because it was warm and exquisitely soft. She'd never owned cashmere. Sadly, the sweater had very tiny moth holes across the back, which were not obvious until she wore it. I asked her if she'd like a new sweater, but she explained how new cashmere is overpriced – ridiculous at best. She'd rather throw the sweater away and find something more conventional in cotton or wool. I believed her. She's a woman of passion and conviction. I knew better than to spend our money on foolish fashion.

How the story managed to take its O'Henry twist is difficult to say. You see, I decided the desk would be nice, so I ordered one of those discounted products made of pressed sawdust from the jungles of industrial China off the Internet site we'd scouted. I even told Pam that I went ahead and ordered it, and she smiled, said she was glad. That evening I talked with a good friend on the phone and she asked if I had any ideas about what Pam might like for Christmas. I mentioned the demise of her cashmere sweater, copied its size surreptitiously off the tag in the rag bag where it ended up, and speculated on the color, a kind of burnt orange. She thanked me for the idea. I smiled.

When the desk arrived, I unpacked the box, got my screwdriver and hex wrench (the only two tools required for assembly) and went to work, erecting my ivory tower. I had to drill a pilot hole where the Chinese had missed one, but overall it assembled nicely and I had a new desk to sit beside in the warmer climate of our living room. It was almost perfect, except for one detail: I couldn't get my knees under it. I had carefully measured the space in the living room before ordering it, but only the distance between the propane stove and the wall. It would fit, I remember telling myself, with a few inches to spare. What I hadn't checked is if I would fit.

When the cashmere sweater arrived, wrapped beautifully in a box with a bright ribbon, I put it under the desk with all the other presents. You see, I had decided to decorate the desk with lights, since it was rather pointless as a desk. On Christmas Eve she unwrapped her present and her eyes grew wide as she held up what could have doubled for an extralarge, bright orange cashmere hunting vest. I covered my face to keep from laughing. She glanced at me with suspicion in her eyes.

Since then the sweater has been exchanged for a gift certificate, and the desk has been turned into a small bookcase near the door. In our household we have resolved to give up trying to surprise each other. Personally, I am working on reducing the number of times I end up surprising myself.

CHAPTER TWELVE

You've got pee-mail

New Year's Day, after the dinner hour, my wife and I prepared for a stroll, intending to wear off a rather generous helping of food. The neighbor's dog watched us from the edge of his driveway as we stepped out the door, anxious to accompany us as he had on almost every other occasion.

We opened our gate, as usual, and the dog rushed through it. After running a little to get his batteries charged up, he stopped to sniff and lift his leg on a fence post. Then it dawned on me that in a sort of low-tech but utterly efficient manner the dog was actually out with us to pick up his pee-mail.

Human beings, for the most part, believe they've been given dominion over the beasts, partly because of our alleged superior intelligence. Animals, however, have for centuries possessed a means of communicating with each other over long distances without paying a monthly user fee.

The concept is not that difficult to follow. I'm surprised I hadn't noticed until now. Think about what's necessary to send and receive messages and you'll see what I mean.

Initially, the animals need a provider, a server if you will. That's where human beings come into the picture. Countless dogs and cats subscribe to the notion, choosing households that function as providers, and thus the pets have cleverly equipped themselves with access to their own version of an information infrastructure.

Naturally, animals are born with the necessary hardware and encryption codes to personalize their locations, combined with a browser that we have for centuries mistaken for a nose. With these minimal requirements fulfilled, the loyal beasts we have thought of as simple pets transform themselves into sophisticated surfers of an organic network, all for as little as a scent.

Our cat learned to use the toilet by reading our pee-mail. You see, living in the Southwest, my wife and I realized long ago the necessity of conserving water, so we don't flush the toilet after each and every pee. I had seen the cat up on the toilet seat on numerous occasions, but I wasn't worried: The cat wasn't going to drink from a contaminated toilet. The cat was smarter than that, and the tinkle I repeatedly heard in the middle of the night was not a dripping faucet. Once again, it took me longer to figure out what the cat was doing than it took the cat to figure out what we were doing. In deference to the cat, we're still responsible for flushing.

I realize now, only in retrospect, that I had already used what the animals know, several years ago when my wife and I were camping in bear country. Locals warned us that the bears were bold and overly familiar with a human presence. That evening, after setting up our tent in the backcountry, I lingered outside by the campfire while Pam went inside the tent to get ready for bed.

It was a lovely night, bright moonlight and stars plentiful as popcorn in a big bowl of summer sky. I'd almost forgotten about the bears until I heard a strange grumble from somewhere off in the dark woods.

Before going to bed, I decided to pee at each of the four corners of the tent, careful of course not to pee on the tent itself. While I stood peeing I concentrated on the bears, as if by telepathy trying to warn them to stay away from our tent.

We woke that night to the sound of some large animal crashing through the undergrowth; we listened tensely, but the animal veered away from our tent and disappeared until all we heard was the static of crickets. Both of us stayed wrapped in our sleeping bags, speechless, but secretly I knew my pee-mail had saved us.

In all likelihood there is animal pee on at least one of your car's tires. Sure, you'd prefer to ignore it, but while you're driving along, talking business on your cell phone with a customer or client who lives across town, realize that you are also the means by which some animal is doing its business. You are like a mobile transmitter generating radial waves, wireless communication, a means by which dogs and cats have sent messages across town ever since Henry Ford pushed his first Model A into the street.

Perhaps I've said enough – maybe even too much.

Lately the neighbor's dog has been acting strangely, sticking uncharacteristically close as we take our walks instead of chasing the usual rabbits out of hiding. He also started playing fetch with a surprising amount of vigor that suggests he's trying to keep me occupied, distracted. I can't imagine what he's heard about us, but I suspect it has to do with the way I tilt my head and look at him whenever he stops to pee.

CHAPTER THIRTEEN

The nose knows

I'd checked out an internet site for advice before setting the trap, baiting it using pieces of apple smeared with peanut butter. The bait looked good enough to eat. Actually, I ate one slice before setting the remainder behind the trigger plate. Skunks are also (according to the internet) especially fond of canned fish, but I preferred apples. If this skunk was going to spend time under my trailer, then it would have to adjust.

The trap itself consisted of a wire cage – a live trap – into which the skunk would be encouraged to stroll, as if entering a restaurant to check on the daily special. There it would be caught and, if all worked according to my plan, transported to a more skunk friendly location. Everything was in place. All I had to do was try to take shallow breaths while inside my home, and be patient.

I must say that during the short time I spent with my skunk I learned more about skunks in general than the internet could share. My skunk was a spotted skunk, not the usual white-stripe-down-the-middle-of-a-black-highway variety. My skunk preferred spraying under my trailer at 5 a.m. on a lazy Sunday morning, prompting me to open all the doors and windows. My skunk waited until I had to teach school on Monday morning to let me know that it, too, would eat apples. I guess we bonded somewhere between the pre-dawn of Sunday when we first met and the pre-dawn of Monday morning, at which time I knew my skunk definitely had to go.

I ignored the quarry in my trap and went to work, aware that my skunk would be lonely and scared, confined to its wire cell under the front deck until late in the afternoon. This delay before it would once again experience freedom couldn't be helped. Truthfully, I felt trapped myself, pacing my classroom, planning how to avoid being sprayed when I tried to drag the trap out from under the deck and place it in the bed of my truck, then again when I released the skunk into the wild. We were of different species but of one mind. For both of us, life temporarily stunk.

When I got home from work I found an old ratty blanket in the garage to throw over the trap. I impersonated a magician conjuring a trick, concentrating on a spell that would make the skunk disappear. I started the truck and drove for miles to what I'll refer to here as an undisclosed location. I don't want any game officers alerted and besides, a skunk demands its privacy, too.

Once I placed the trap on the ground, off toward a thick patch of tall brown grass, I wedged a stick into a slot so the door would stay open. I stepped back, way back. And I waited. Five minutes elapsed before the skunk's nose made its first appearance, sniffing around the perimeter of the door.

At last, I thought, my skunk has caught the scent of freedom. When it was fully emerged from the trap, I waved my arms like a runway attendant high on jet fumes. Go, I urged. Live once more. The skunk taxied a 360 and scurried back inside the trap! This went on for 20 minutes, in and out, in and out. I never realized how difficult it is to reverse one's in-stink.

So I tied a long cord to the trap and from a distance snatched it away once the skunk emerged. What should have been applauded as the work of a genius turned into a disaster, for as soon as my skunk saw its cover vanish, it scrambled across the parking lot gravel and climbed swiftly into the rear wheel well of my truck. I kid you not. It found a cranny between the box metal and literally disappeared.

No matter how much racket I made jumping up and down in the bed of the truck or how patiently I waited beside the tall grass, my skunk refused to show itself. I started the truck and gunned the engine, which only reminded me that I did, after all, own a gun.

Eventually the sun headed for its nest on the horizon, but I stood in the cold, too far away from my home to walk there. And if I drove my truck home the skunk, a nocturnal creature, would no doubt climb down from the wheel well and return to its familiar nook under my trailer. Deja vu is one thing, but deja phew I can live without.

In the end I had no choice: I drove my truck back to town, parked it at another undisclosed location and walked a short distance to a good friend's house. He would understand, I told myself. He wouldn't laugh at me.

He laughed. He wanted to hear the entire story, twice. Then he drove me home and even came back the next morning to pick me up and drop me at the spot where I'd parked my truck overnight. The windshield held a thick layer of ice, which he helped me scrape before getting into his own truck, laughing once more, and driving away.

I started the engine. The exhaust produced a cloud of vapor that hung in the still morning air. My skunk had, at last, departed, leaving me with a whiff of what I suspected to be my dignity.

CHAPTER FOURTEEN

Birds with few feathers

Long-necked llamas have made a home in the West for some time now. You'd recognize a llama at first glance, I know you would. Ogden Nash, decades ago, penned a little poem to help anyone who couldn't distinguish between the beast and the lama that's a priest. I won't repeat it for you here because I don't want to be sued out of my silk pajamas. Still, I mention the llama, because it's time for a new rhyme celebrating a creature from Australia that hasn't been had much luck making a home with ranchers in the West. I'm speaking of the emu. So here it is, my contribution to the annals of animal verse:

> *You'd think an emu is a bird*
> *But like an ostrich, it's absurd.*
> *And if an emu learned to fly*
> *You'd duck fast as the other guy.*

Truthfully, I'd never thought of joining a bird rodeo until the evening before Thanksgiving, while my wife and I were walking along the irrigation canal that stretches just east of our house. Normally we see a few rabbits, birds, skunks, an occasional deer and quite a few healthy snakes. The landfill is only a half-mile from our house and the wildlife around us is not that wild. We get a lot of scavengers looking for municipal handouts. If we had to survive by hunting, we'd eat a lot of crow. This emu, though, was a bird of a different feather.

A neighbor drove up in his truck and pulled over, rolled down his window, pointed and told us he'd tried to approach the bird when he first noticed it in his yard, but it began stomping its two enormous prehensile feet in a very hostile manner. Touring the neighborhood in his truck, he asked area residents without any luck if anyone knew where an emu might roost. No one knew what to make of an emu. One local swore that a disgruntled emu rancher had loosed the last six of his herd (if you can call more than one bird a herd) into the hills to fend for themselves. He knew what to make of an emu: Shoot it and cook it. With this comment served up as the collective wisdom of our neighborhood, the bird's future was looking dim as the sun faded, this evening before Thanksgiving. I volunteered to call the authorities.

It was after five o'clock. I spoke with answering machines for the Humane Society and the Animal Control office. Funny, the way answering machines don't really have any answers. I got two busy signals before finally getting through to the police department's non-emergency operator. I was transferred to a dispatcher who listened to my story but said no police officer would be able to apprehend an emu. Though I hadn't witnessed our jailbird's attempt at flight, I knew the dispatcher was right. She, in turn, assured me that I shouldn't worry, that the animal would find its way home eventually, because people out in my neighborhood only shoot stray dogs.

I got to worrying anyway, wondering about emus, thinking I should know something about what they eat, how they shelter, how they defend themselves in a hostile world. I couldn't take the bird home. I didn't even know if it was a female or an emale. It was going to be a cold night and I half-suspected I'd have to thaw the bird by morning if it chose to stay in the grass beside the canal. I went home to do a little research.

An emu (pronounced "ee-mew") turns out to be a sole surviving species from Australia. It is the largest of flightless birds, next to the ostrich. An emu can attain the height of 6 feet and weigh 130 lbs. I knew if we could train them to play basketball, the public would appreciate emus more. I was also beginning to understand why ranchers were interested in emu. Their meat is low in cholesterol, high in protein, and even tastes great! So why aren't people flocking to the supermarket for a few pounds of ground emu?

The bird, as a visual experience, is a tragedy. Though it can move gracefully at speeds very frustrating to its potential predators, it stands in a field like a ballerina in cowboy boots. It's difficult to imagine how birds in general are the closest genetic link we have with extinct dinosaurs, but it's impossible for an emu to deny its ancestry. Strangely, the bird is described as being peaceful and timid, interested in grazing on fruits, seeds, and flowers. I called a woman nearby who used to raise emus to apprise her of the emu situation near my house. She said her family butchered their remaining stock and had no plans to hatch a new enterprise. Emus, according to this exemu rancher, have nasty dispositions and their marketable worth has plummeted to practically nothing.

Thanksgiving morning while I struggled to get into my own dressing, my wife was in the kitchen stuffing the turkey. She suggested as I headed out the door, "Take a pail of that field corn I keep in the garage."

When I arrived at the spot where I'd last seen the emu, it looked as docile as an undetonated hand grenade. I approached and tossed a handful of corn in front of me. The emu stepped back. When I looked up, I saw a man walking across the field, swinging a lariat. Here was someone I hoped knew a little more about an emu than me.

He spoke with a thick Spanish dialect, a transplant into the English-speaking world, and he explained how this emu was practically a pet that he kept in a field with his sheep, but two days ago it escaped. He spied the corn and said his emu loved corn, but that he'd run out, had to feed it oats, which the emu didn't appreciate. I tossed down a little more corn and the emu cautiously approached, then it gave in to an old pleasure: Eating cuisine.

Every time my little neighbor tossed his lasso, the emu skillfully evaded the noose and sped off along the fence line. After nearly a dozen attempts, my five-foot two-inch neighbor managed to toss a loop over the bird's head and we pulled the bird to the ground, the emu kicking, floundering, struggling with its powerful legs and useless wings to get loose. Suddenly I was glad I didn't own an emu. Though this was the first emu rodeo I'd competed in, I knew right off why people would not eat this bird. I was also confident they wouldn't try to put a saddle on it.

We finally managed to get my neighbor's hat pulled

over the emu's head and it calmed the bird enough so we could wrap the rope around its legs and roll its body through an opening in the barbed wire fence. Only then did we dare let the emu stand upright again. We didn't stand there for long. Suddenly the emu dragged my partner off toward his home while he glanced back over his shoulder, smiling and waving. I watched the two of them disappear in this awkward dance across the field, each taking turns at yanking the other, as if the cosmos had become a giant yo-yo where it was impossible to tell who controlled the string.

CHAPTER FIFTEEN

Breaking for freedom in the New West

My neighbor owns a horse. I see it standing in the field across from my house every morning as I leave for work, and when I come home the same horse is still waiting there, like a picture of grace and power that has no place to go.

My neighbor rides the horse up the road and back again on weekends, a sort of cowboy without a cow, horsepower enough to rustle a few moments from the week, then turn them loose before heading back to his modern life at the doublewide ranch.

I could theoretically be his partner, for I watch him – even watch for him – as he rides up the road, and somehow feel an affinity for his refusal to sell the animal or let somebody put the old horse out to pasture. Oh, we're a sorry bunch, Easterners and Midwesterners transplanted in the West, imagining an eternal frontier.

We see the mountains rise up like so many bucking broncos, hunker down beside a side-winding river, and we're forever romantic, cellular phones and paging devices flashing in the holsters strapped to our belts. And the real Westerners, the few around us, the ones born in the valley and nursed on a secret formula of chewing tobacco and beer, they think the only reason strangers keep showing up is because someone forgot to close the gate.

My neighbor doesn't care what people think. It's obvious to anyone who drives past: His yard is a clutter of junk cars, broken appliances, twisted bicycle frames, and iron parts from something unnatural that seems to have planted itself as a memorial.

His horse has a little piece of ground fenced off from the chaos, its own grass, bathtub trough, and a good view of the mountains. Granted, it's not much, but how much does a horse need? A cowboy, on the other hand, has to keep his stock in line, and though my neighbor's horse doesn't appear to get as much attention as his pickup truck, boat, camper, snowmobiles, or his ATV, it stands as an idle reminder that we, too, can be saddled by whatever holds the reins.

Everything I own eats a little of my time, even if it claims to save it in the long run. My car guzzles gas, my computer consumes bytes of information, my telephone beeps and swallows half a dozen voices only to regurgitate them when I finally get home. My DVR records the shows I don't have time to watch so I can view them once I've pulled an hour free, just like an old farmer clearing his land, tree by tree.

Last year my neighbor's horse suddenly bolted through a barbed wire fence. Two deep gashes were torn into its chest as well as a multitude of smaller ones across its front legs. The horse might have died – would have died – but my neighbor caught it, and because he owns no stable or shed where he might confine a horse, he came to me to ask if he might use my garage.

There, he tied the horse to the front wall and with no more than a quick injection of veterinarian Novocain, began to stitch the horse's flesh together using a curved needle he'd packed away with his experience as a medic in Vietnam. I'd never seen anything like it, except to watch my grandmother stitch a quilt in her lap, but here were blood, tissue, and muscle exposed like so many anatomy schematics in a textbook, things that belonged on the inside somehow laid open.

My neighbor put all the parts back and shut the fleshy door, the entire time complaining about how much hay a horse can put away in one winter. As he led his horse out, I suddenly knew how such a placid animal could have behaved so rashly, charging a barbed wire fence.

The last time it happened to me, I wound up in western Colorado.

But I was pulling a trailer packed tight with a few hundred necessities. I unpacked them all, took a deep breath of that clear Western air, and started planning where I'd teach school next.

I'd like to think that that horse and me are some kind of kin – patient, yet yearning for the unbridled life. We make our halfhearted breaks for freedom, searching for a slightly different perspective of that same old mountain.

Meanwhile, another year begins, and we keep on plugging.

section two

Remodeling Eden

CHAPTER SIXTEEN

Sub-di-vi-sions

Genesis asserts the universe was created in six stages. If I accept this account, then the Garden of Eden qualifies as the earth's first subdivision. Strictly speaking, the tenants violated some sort of unwritten lease or covenant agreement, resulting in their eviction. Since then, real estate may have evolved but precedents have been established.

I have no light to shed on these Biblical arrangements, but I would like to say something about the subdivision itself. What perplexes me is that anyone would choose to move away from Eden, especially when immortality comes with it, a perk nobody can live without.

When I compare what's marketed today, however, to that first subdivision, I confess I am a little disappointed. It's the sin of unoriginality that depresses me. Current developers lack the imagination not only to design low-profile, efficient, and artistically crafted homes, but they can't even come up with decent names for their communities.

More than likely, once the county commissioners approve a landowner's request for a permit to build a subdivision, I suppose the major partners in the deal buy an undisclosed quantity of beer and sit somewhere nearby, conjuring all sorts of images to chisel into a stone slab beside the entrance gate.

"Whadaya wanna call this place?" Adam Jr. asks.

"Sure got some purdy views," Evie replies.

No doubt they stare at the sky where a vinyl window will one day materialize, remembering their mothers' names, their favorite sports teams, their best dogs, or even their first loves. In the end, though, it comes down to a generic, uninspired agreement not to rock the boat of cliches, the predictably predictable nomenclature of subdivisions.

I'm still imagining this, but I suppose a building code requires developers to use two roulette-style wheels, with a limited vocabulary painted on plywood. After the first six-pack, the wheels are rotated. One of the wheels, at least based on the subdivision signs I've seen, lists an array of organic nomenclature, like flowers, plants, shrubs, or trees. On the other wheel, an armada of geologic formations appears. When both wheels are nudged simultaneously, they spin and the jackpot spells out a two word combination. After a 12-pack it must read like an inspiration.

Pinon Hills, Cedar Mesa, Cottonwood Butte. The platitudes coat the tongue like sour milk. Pinon Butte, Cedar Hills, Cottonwood Canyons – cliches, exciting as warm spit. Of course, the intellectuals add verbs and get combinations like Whispering Pines, Echo Canyon, or Rolling Meadows. Believe me, if I had to live in a subdivision that people referred to by any of these trite names, I'd feel morally obligated to sneak outside late at night and rotate their signs. I mean, really, if these are the signs of our times, then these times are destined to be studied by future generations as the Pathetic Era.

A good name offers a place its soul. If profit margins and marketability are the major motivations behind creating communities in the Southwest, then I understand why I'm living in a landscape of transients, a collection of unsettled wanderers searching for a place that feels like home. When I lived in England, I marveled at the Brits' ability to litter their lives with clever identifiers. I ate dinner at The Whim, consumed Bubble and Squeak, drank beer at The Quiet Woman (illustrated on the marque by a headless woman, holding her head under her arm), and tried not to sigh while standing on the Bridge of Sighs. I came away from my international travel experience believing a culture can possess the power to bestow significance by choosing proper and witty names.

Of course, living with a woman who can't buy a toaster without christening it hasn't hurt. I'll admit that not every name she chooses strikes me as perfect, especially when her label-maker is pointed at me. I have been (lovingly) referred to (in public) by pet names which include pooker puppy, bunny rabbit, and snake lips. These synonyms for my name twist off her tongue as sweetly as red licorice, but I've also watched many eyebrows raise as people who thought they knew me stare at me in a new way.

I know it's not a simple task to find the right name. Sometimes you have to wait for the name to come to you. When I moved into my house 20 years ago, my neighbor, an old farmer, came to my door dangling a four foot bull snake by its tail, telling me how it was the solution to my infestation of rattlers. I cautiously thanked him and asked him to let the snake go, which he did, and it slithered away under the trailer. I wondered how he managed to catch it.

"Up here on Turkey Buzzard Hill," my neighbor said, "ya gotta be quick." And he smiled, turned, and headed down the driveway toward his home.

Later that evening, I told Pam how our neighbor had delivered our property's name along with a bull snake. She nodded, unintimidated by snakes, indicating the name would suit her fine.

"Is it male or female?"

"The neighbor?" I asked.

"The snake!"

"I didn't have the courage to check," I admitted.

"Then we'll call it Herman," she said, "A name befitting the undisclosed gender, one word containing two references, both female and male."

I nodded, indicating the name would suit me fine.

"That is," she replied, "until you have the courage to check."

Chapter Seventeen

Summer homes, some ain't

Memorial Day had arrived and graveyards all across America were being decorated with wreaths, sprays, and garlands. Pam and I expected a low impact holiday, without any real plans in the works. No relatives stopping over, no picnics, nothing memorial...that is, until Pam had her "idea."

Her idea amounted to driving across Lizard Head Pass, through the valley of fruit and corn, and eventually ending up at the old town of Redstone. We had been through this tiny mining, now tourist town many times while camping in the national forest, but we'd never stayed overnight at the historic Redstone Inn. Supposedly, it's haunted.

We arrived as planned, a few days before the rate increase for summer tourists. A dormer room on the third floor offered a toilet and sink but no tub or shower. These amenities were down the hall, shared with other third floor guests, which is why our rent was affordable. We unpacked our bags and stretched our legs by taking a walk through town before settling in for the night.

The only street in Redstone runs about a half mile, perfectly straight, with no fewer than five speed bumps evenly spaced along the way. During the height of tourist season, the speed bumps probably slow gawking tourists down, but on this day the center of the street served us well, with no fear of traffic. Local shops and residences occupy each side of the street, many of them the historic remnants of a turn-of-the-century social experiment sponsored by the town's founder, John Cleveland Osgood, a wealthy coal industrialist from the East. Mr. Osgood believed that if workers could be provided decent housing, they would be "less troublesome."

The Inn had been built at the south end of the street to lodge the town's bachelors, while families were provided with small, tastefully designed cottages. It's an attractive town even today, but when we visited many businesses were still closed and some of the immaculate half-million dollar "cottages" that had been tastefully renovated by present day homeowners were still locked, shuttered, and empty. It felt like a ghost town.

Actual ghosts don't worry me much. What bothers me the most is that many of the people who supposedly live here hadn't yet materialized. They were the real ghosts, residents who pay their taxes and disappear for the better part of the year, inflating property values and creating a community of absentee opinions.

I've never owned two or three residences, living at one location, then hopping to another when the weather turns hospitable, but multiple home ownership is happening all across the West. Finding a room for the night that's under a hundred bucks is more than enough paranormal activity for me.

And all that remains of Redstone's social experiment is the skeleton of its intent. Redstone is not the only town inhabited by the apparition of wealth. Telluride has an entire village that stays eerily empty once the skiers have gone home, then there's Aspen, Vail, Steamboat Springs, and the greater Phoenix area. Hopefully another ghost village proposed for the top of Wolf Creek Pass will simply vanish. It's just spooky when I try to count my neighbors and it's virtually impossible to see them.

I stayed up late after we got back to our room, and when I reached up to turn out the light over our bed, I thought I heard a sigh. It was only Pam, glad I'd finally decided to go to sleep. I settled in, pulled the covers up, roughed up a pillow until it adjusted to the shape of my skull. Then something happened to set both of us suddenly upright in our bed, wide-eyed and staring at each other: The light came on by itself, both bulbs burning bright.

I knew Pam hadn't turned it on, because she'd been half asleep when I turned it off. And it wasn't me. I looked around the room, then reached up once more and turned the switch off. The room stayed dark this time, but I swear only one of us was breathing.

CHAPTER EIGHTEEN

Buying used gets me enthused

Westerners are packrats. Blame it on the availability of flea markets, or just the size of our backyards. My house is no exception, except that most of my stuff comes from the midden heap, which doesn't mean I've been pilfering artifacts from sacred sites.

The Anasazi used to dump their trash much like many of our ranchers, farmers, and land owners – into the nearest arroyo – which archaeologists have taken to calling "midden heaps." In a thousand years whoever digs up my ruin will find more than they bargained for.

The midden heap I refer to has been sponsored by a local thrift store. I'm proud to live in this region, because the West is a haven for us fix-it up types, folks who don't throw anything away, because one day it might come in handy. Maybe I ought to have been an archaeologist. I own enough stuff to open my own museum, but I lack the training to properly classify and display it.

My mother was appalled when she first learned that I shop at thrift stores. To her and many of her generation, thrift stores were full of dead people's clothes, where the destitute shuffled in for a handout. She insisted on buying her stuff new. I try to think of a thrift store as an excavation. The goods arrive, usually in a mound at the back door, and savvy sorters begin by digging through the bags and boxes to separate what's saleable from what belongs in the dumpster.

During this process the workers can be heard to exclaim, Look at this! Or, What the heck is that supposed to be? When archaeologists can't identify an artifact, they pass it off as having "sacred or religious" significance Luckily the volunteers don't write dissertations about their quandaries. They simply shrug their shoulders, laugh, and set it out on a shelf to see if a customer can identify it.

I never realized how much of the world gets discarded. Everything new can suddenly turn less than new, less than perfect. Once upon a time, thrift shops were havens of the poor, those down on their luck or just plain downtown, looking for a drink. The Salvation Army, The Goodwill, New Horizons. Names flying like flags where we pledge our sympathy.

I've seen people in the aisles, holding a shirt up against a shadow, fitting a foot into a shoe they'd like to fill. Others are families, mothers with children in tow, furiously shopping so they might fill an empty bag. College kids laughing outrageously at what looks outrageous. Then buying it.

Pioneers settled the West, spurred by the thrill of discovery, and it's exciting to know that the thrill hasn't vanished. Last week, I found a car rack for my mountain bike at a thrift store, identical to the $60 version I bought at a specialized bike shop. The used one cost me 3 bucks, so instead of owning two, I returned the expensive one for a refund. I've purchased furniture with no down payment, and the only interest I have to deal with comes from the people who stop by and ask, "Wherever did you find that chair?"

I've got more used books than I'll ever be able to read in one lifetime, but when I heard that bookshelves in a double-wide make excellent insulation, I get a warm feeling every time I buy another.

Some people might call what I do cheap, but I'm comfortable with the word. Compare the thrifty feeling with the typical advertising banter of blowout sales at most retail stores and you'll understand why "used" gets me enthused. I mean, really, a 15 percent savings on Levi jeans! Big deal. The relaxed fit I'm after is the knowledge that my total bill adds up to an average mall shopper's sales tax.

You see, there's nothing wrong with secondhand. So much of what we use hardly ever gets used up. When we learn to feel at home with what has been in other people's homes, we begin to see the West as a great recycling bin – not just a receptacle for glass, aluminum, paper, or plastic.

As thrifters, we are born into the ranks of gold diggers or even tinhorn sheriffs, the ones who ask the rustler with the noose around his neck what he intends to do with his boots once he's ridden into the unknown.

CHAPTER NINETEEN

Bulldozer diplomacy

'd decided to take a hike on our land south of town, a narrow strip an acre wide and 11 acres deep. Pam said she'd come along, she needed the break. I was glad, I needed the company. In the 18 years we lived together on this property we'd done literally nothing with the bulk of acreage except wear a footpath around its perimeter. The land was home to birds, deer, skunks, rabbits, dogs, mountain lions, feral cats, juniper, piñon, a few cottonwoods along the irrigation canal, and sage – acres of sage, most of it waist high and thick as a picket fence.

I couldn't help thinking of Moses when we came upon the spot where the usual sage suddenly parted like the Red Sea. Of course, in the desert Southwest there isn't enough water for such a miracle, but a path as wide as a bulldozer had been gouged out of our property. As we stepped into the clearing we saw dozer tracks pressed into the dirt. I scratched my head.

"I'm no Sherlock," Pam said, "but I think we should follow them."

So follow the tracks we did, and they weren't difficult to follow. Even if I'd been a private detective from the Clovis point era, I'd have likened our quest to stalking a dinosaur. The tracks took us out to the gravel county road and looped back toward a neighbor's land that bordered a section along our western property line. We walked up the driveway and knocked on the door.

"Yeah?"

"I thought you might be able to explain to us why you had a bulldozer on our property?" I said.

"Who told you I had anything to do with a bulldozer?" Obviously, the man was still trying to bulldoze us.

I pointed toward the road. "Nobody told us anything, but we followed tracks, ending at your driveway."

"Who are you?" he asked, changing his line of inquiry.

"We're your neighbors, the people who own the property to the east."

"Nobody owns that," he declared, "It's BLM property."

"Actually, if it were BLM property, the public owns it and it would still be illegal to bulldoze public land."

"Well, I'm a member of the public." He flashed us a toothy smile.

"Well, we're the property owners," I shot back. "And nice to meet you," I added, just to counterpoint an awkward situation.

I could hear his steel treads beginning to seize. Then he ran out of diesel and just gave up, admitted to his mischief, and claimed he really didn't know, that he worried about not having a back gate on his property. We said we understood (although we didn't) and asked him to fill his gouge (hopefully with grey matter) and repair the ruined fence (wishing, of course, he could replace the sage). He agreed to everything and we shook hands.

He also agreed to nothing, for I'm as certain today as I was so many years ago that if he had the chance, he'd do it again. The idea that land remains in the public trust gives him permission to abuse it, according to his ilk, and that includes the right to dig pots and artifacts, shoot bullets through signs, dump garbage into arroyos, and toss litter – including beer cans and bottles – out the windows of moving vehicles. He is privileged to live in America where land is preserved in his name, but all he thinks is that he is privileged.

As we walked back home we promised ourselves to scout our property line more often, to keep a closer eye on The Public.

"You know," I said to Pam, "now that we've been designated BLM, I don't see why we should be paying property taxes."

She looked at me and smiled, then she took my hand and we continued along our hiking trail until we reached the house. Along the way we didn't see any other hikers, which is good, because I've been thinking about implementing a user fee program for the neighbor's kids, just in case they want a piece of this public land experience.

CHAPTER TWENTY

Natural preserves

We were out for a Sunday drive in the country, but we hadn't packed a lunch. Instead, my father loaded three empty pails in the trunk, said they'd be full by the time we returned home.

He gave me what he called an optometrist's wink: It meant, I'd see. Within an hour we were standing beside each other on a rural gravel road. I could see nothing except green leaves and a billow of dust settling like a rough burlap sack.

When I first looked up and noticed the clusters of purplish red berries, I thought, what a magical place, where fruit grows like this by the side of the road so anyone can stop and fill a bucket with sweetness. Then I popped a couple berries in my mouth and dropped my bucket, spitting a wad of pulpy pits at the dirt: My first taste of chokecherries.

Naturally, it took some time for me to try the vile berry again, even after my mother rinsed and cooked the chokecherries down to mush, squeezed the pulp, added sugar, boiled the concoction again, ladled the brilliantly royal syrup into jars she had also boiled, then melted a pan of paraffin to seal a dozen jars like a hive full of bright red honey.

"It's really good," she urged with a spoon hovering in the air.

I resisted, the memory powerful enough to pucker my lips again, the shock of looking down at my hands covered with fruit blood from stripping cluster after cluster into a steel bucket. Chokecherries, indeed!

Some things acquire their fondness with time and in spite of my childishness – maybe even to catch hold of that child again? – I now harvest the roadsides whenever I can. These days it's my wife, riding shotgun and scanning the ditches, who encourages me. Now, of course, I worry about signs that threaten trespassers, ranchers with shotguns, reckless drivers, poison ivy, even toxic roadside sprays, but something spurs me on. Maybe it's the element of risk in the pursuit of roadside bounty, or the serendipity of finding what looks abandoned. Or maybe it's a primitive vein the color of sunset running buried in us from the days when we hunted and gathered just to survive.

We've discovered a brimming bounty here where we live. On our roadside foraging expeditions, we've encountered apricots, apples, peaches, grapes, asparagus, raspberries, wild strawberries, rose hips, a few plums, and, naturally, those memorable chokecherries.

To leave them for the animals and birds might make environmental sense, but no grocery store on earth can replicate the same wild taste. Maybe it's the road dust or the way the sun radiates off the road surface that ripens this produce in a unique way. Or it's my mother's voice, still caught somewhere inside me, telling me that it's really good.

I can't explain why, I can only stop.

It's popular among writers today to memorialize natural wonders and wilderness, urging readers to preserve our land, to celebrate an ecologically sound way of thinking about the earth. It's no surprise, then, that back roads have become valued as a way to travel the countryside, to see what lies off the beaten path. But can a nation of consumers, often likened to swarms of locust, ever really savor these resources without destroying them?

I have a plan. Along every roadside in the West – even those blasted interstates – are public easements, spaces preserved for the access of public utilities. In these roadside public lands, we should plant fruit trees and shrubs that produce an abundance of edible things.

And why stop there? Down with sod and gravel, and the corporate privatization of America. Down with zoning land to be covered with rivers of asphalt and concrete. Tell the shopping malls you want fruit trees planted in their parking lots. Better yet, don't tell: Sneak out at night and put in some huckleberries along a section of storm sewer or culvert. Check your region and growing season in a seed catalog and buy a few drought resistant varieties of fruit that will take hold of the earth and root deep in this country's memory. And why adopt a highway just to pick up litter? Become a Johnny Anyseed, planting to produce a bounty of sweet things.

Of course there'll be a bureaucratic sourpuss somewhere telling you fruit is far too messy, that trees and shrubs need to be pruned, that the plan, as I have outlined it, needs to be regulated by official approvals and clearances. The world is perennial in its ability to produce people who mature like clusters of bitter chokecherries.

Persist, though, and we can again turn earth back into an Eden where no fruit will ever be forbidden.

CHAPTER TWENTY-ONE

The long view

On the longest day of the year when sunlight puddles at the horizon, it's officially summer. Every year from such a precipice we call the solstice, the long ascent and the long decline are equally visible. Maybe that's why there's so much light, and so much extra time to see.

A beautiful sunset and a warm evening will conjure my red 1965 Mustang convertible every time. Just the thought of it makes me close my eyes. Like light from a burned-out star, all that flashy chrome still shines from somewhere inside me. All those layers of wax I buffed clean through the hood still make the sweat on my forehead bead up. The top folded back, the radio blaring, a full summer moon rolling like a hubcap across the sky.

I was 18 years old. A senior in high school, majoring in myself. My hair was longer than my father liked it, my face was blemished with self doubt, as if my sense of imperfection constantly wanted out. My mother reminded me not to slouch, then opened the plate glass door to the office where she worked and ushered me through it.

"Don't be disappointed if she already sold it," my mother coached. "And don't look excited if she hasn't, at least until I've had a chance to ask how much she wants."

I waited in the hall. I stared at my feet until I noticed how the linoleum sent back a ghostly, wavering silhouette of my own body. I studied my reflection, leaning into it. From my mother's point of view, I was slouching. But I swear I caught a glimpse of the future in that shine, like in a crystal ball, I was consulting the powers of fate and fortune, I was tuned in to the pulse and strobe of fluorescent lighting that stretched across the ceiling. I was coming down like a pilot toward a landing strip, wings balanced, the ground seeming to rise, the runway crew scrambling to welcome me with wild arms.

Nobody owns the road, but put a teenager in the driver's seat and he thinks he does. I was, in the flick of an ignition switch, a devout convert to the temple of the industrial world. I would kneel at its altar all spring, anointed to the elbows with grease from a hundred graveyard shifts in a downtown Minneapolis machine shop, where my paycheck was a cache of power: Horsepower.

When I pulled out of my parents' driveway, I was in charge. Nobody told me what I should or should not do, what to think, when to sit, speak, or in what particular tone of voice I was or was not supposed to address them. With the top down, I listened to the harmony of the spheres transmitted through my cylinders. I stepped on the accelerator and made my 289 cubic inches howl back at the moon.

That was, as they say, then. Here is closer to now: My Mustang is gone, traded for a year of college tuition. I don't even remember the face that came to pay for the car or pick it up. Man or woman, I don't really know. Human — at least human — I can assure you. I lived in a basement with three roommates and I was authentically on my own for the first time in my life, flagrantly disconnected from my family and the college's dormitory system, a rebel without a car. Every responsibility in the world came down on me, but I couldn't see them coming: Rent, the telephone bill (with long-distance charges by a room-mate who moved away), groceries, even dog food, despite the reality that the dog I fed didn't belong to me.

Here is now again, almost free of nostalgia: I'm still in charge, no boss threatening me with termination, that is, unless retirement and cholesterol count as bosses. I used to be an English teacher in a small high school two thousand miles from my hometown. I'm still happily married, with IRAs, and driving a hybrid. My Mustang would be priceless if I still owned it. I have no children, my mother and father gone down the road ahead of me.

When I first buckled up in the driver's seat of that Mustang, I thought now was forever. One full tank of gas would have been enough to convince me I had eternal life. Apparently life doesn't get that kind of mileage. You inherit it from someone else, from your parents for instance, and they, in turn, from their parents. It increases in value the longer you have it until near the end you would give anything to have it back, as they say in the blue book, to appreciate.

No doubt I'll go on thinking about my red 1965 Mustang convertible, now that the steel has been dissolved and recast as memory and the memory welded to these words. I'll be retired for 20 years and still wonder if I ever truly was free. It may be that a post-industrial boy's rite of passage is acted out through his machine.

Independence is a spark leaping across a universe that ignites us into being. And here I keep polishing a little spot in time, imagining it forever winking back at me.

CHAPTER TWENTY-TWO

Killing trees with dad

My father led me into the hills one Sunday in December more than 35 years ago. I carried the saw; he carried the axe.

We trudged through the snow, hunting the wild Christmas tree. He checked each tree for fullness and height, trying to picture it standing in our living room beside the couch. I checked the bottom, worried that the stacks of Christmas presents I imagined might not fit underneath.

When we made our selection, my father cut. I shouted "timber" as the tree fell over, then ran around its fallen corpse singing "Ding-Dong the Witch is Dead" instead of an inspirational chorus of "Oh Christmas Tree." My father told me to shut up.

After dragging the tree to our car and tying it to the roof rack, I noticed for the first time my sticky hands. My father said it was just tree sap. I looked at my hands in horror; I glanced at the stump of the tree's trunk where a bead of amber glistened in the sunlight: It was tree blood!

When we got home I went to my room, unwilling to touch that tree again, and – much to my father's dismay – I refused to decorate it. I stayed clear of our tree all during the holidays, only creeping up on it Christmas morning to snatch my presents away.

I hadn't, for some reason, seen a Christmas tree as a living thing until I had, with my father's help, managed to cut one down.

Ever since that fatal Christmas I vowed never to kill another tree for mere decoration. I have cut dead standing trees for firewood and gone to the lumber yard to purchase boards. I have rubbed lemon Pledge on my dining room table and sliced vegetables on a cutting board. But never, never, never will I ever again cut a living tree off the face of this planet for a month of tinsel and lights.

By New Year's Day, Christmas trees have exhausted their usefulness. The needles come loose at the slightest touch; they turn brown and drop to the floor in a futile attempt at fertilizing the carpet. Trees are like that: They never stop trying to do their ecological best to help the planet.

My father dragged the tree out the back door, wrapped in a shroud – or so it seemed – and all the joy it had once embodied for him was somehow drained from it. Drained from us. I don't mean to sound like Scrooge, trashing a tradition simply for the sake of complaining, but wouldn't giving one little gift to the earth be a nice thing to do for Christmas? One little gift from the people who abuse her the most?

94

And I don't mean planting a tree to make up for the one you're taking, though by all means, plant one if you haven't thought of that. No, I mean instead of planting one, leave one grow. No house is better for having a dying tree standing in it. This is a tradition we, as a nation, can do without.

My father tried half-heartedly to revive the tradition of Christmas trees in our house, but the damage was done. There was no way to bring it back to life. Then, one year, he came home with a large cardboard box. Inside was our first artificial tree. Granted, it was an ugly thing, so unlike a real tree that I wondered if the people who manufactured it in China had no trees of their own to use as models.

We kept that tree, though, and every year when we pulled it out of the attic I remembered our expedition to the woods, a place that has become sacred for me, where those beautiful, living, sentient beings called trees are celebrating every day the rebirth of our planet.

CHAPTER TWENTY-THREE

The pavement polka

In the winter of my thirteenth year, my junior high school physical education teacher forced me to dance with a girl. I would have been happier outside, playing hockey, getting knocked on my butt, impressing people who passed by with the accuracy of my snowballs.

The cold weather transformed our gym into a fresh meat storage locker packed with geeky teenagers wearing sweaty gym shorts, T-shirts, and tennis shoes, sharing the intimacies of an infinite moment in the arms of the opposite sex. I didn't have rhythm, I didn't have finesse. I had pimples and slippery palms. The girl, if I remember correctly, fixed me with a look that taught me the meaning of disdain.

Since that time I've avoided traditional dancing altogether, but of all the classic steps drilled into my head, I remember the rhythm of the polka best. A polka is a Bohemian dance done in duple time with a basic pattern of hop-step-close-step. Newcomers would have you believe that the fandango provides a more suitable rhythm for living in the Four Corners, but I beg to differ – you're not a true Westerner until you've mastered the pavement polka.

Step #1: Dance around the potholes but keep in mind that potholes breed potholes. As the cold weather grates its teeth against each road surface, potholes must often be upgraded to craters. The best way to move around them is to stay loose. I recommend a modified tug-swerve-tug-swerve rhythm with your steering wheel. Touch the brake very lightly. You don't want to end up in another driver's arms, a stranger who already has a long term commitment with an insurance company different than your own.

Step #2: Watch out for wildlife. Don't tread on any hooves or paws, demonstrating your clumsiness behind the wheel. Any deer standing near the highway can just as easily be sitting in your lap, if you're not careful. If an intimate drive through the mountains is all you're after, don't confuse a skunk with the white stripe running down the center of the road.

Step #3: Keep an eye out for dangerous curves, and don't be lured by the notion that curves can be attractive. You've seen those drivers who think they've entered the Grand Prix as soon as the road starts to twist. Keep your hips firmly in line with your shoulders. Keep both hands in front of you, gripping the steering wheel. Approach any bend in the road as if it's the one with arthritis.

Step #4: Stay clear of gridlock. I know you think we don't have gridlock in the Four Corners – Denver has gridlock. We live on a relatively peaceful stretch of asphalt. But don't be misled. Construction workers across the Southwest have been assigned the task of frustrating neophytes by idling our time behind a string of motionless vehicles. They use orange cones on the road surfaces just like instructors at the Fred Astaire Dancing School use painted footprints on the dance floor.

Step #5: Avoid falling rocks. If a rock has ever worked itself loose from a mountainside and headed your way, you can't avoid understanding the gravity of the situation. My father-in-law, driving all the way from Chicago, bent his driveshaft coming across Wolf Creek. He hit what he described as a fairly innocent rock as it waited in the center of his lane, prompting his most useful cliche: Take everything you see for granite.

Step #6: Watch out for tourists. There are simply too many Kodak moments where a wide-eyed driver can be Four-Cornered. If you're tailgating, you may get a bit of tail in your teeth. Better to stay back from any vehicle bigger than a pickup truck. Out-of-state license plates are just another way of saying the person in front of you drives to a different drummer. Smile and wave as they cha-cha past. Don't stare at their outfit unless, of course, it's skimpier than the one you are driving.

Step #7: Blend in with the cattle drives. You can't go around them without having to cover a lot more ground than the beef. Try not to feel as if you are being forced into a slow dance. Relax: Listen to the moosic.

Step #8: Emergency vehicles have a way of shaking you out of your reverie with their piercing sirens and flashing lights. It may seem like disco is back, for an instant, but if you'll just pull to the side this too will pass.

Eventually you'll have to shut off the engine and get out of the car. You'll feel a little like Dorothy without her ruby slippers, like Lawrence Welk without his bubble machine. Finally, your feet will be motionless, flat against the ground, but the earth – confound that thing – will continue to spin.

CHAPTER TWENTY-FOUR

Where the recycling ends

Many people donate their discards to area thrift stores, and believe me, the stores are grateful. Donations are their inventory. But what most people don't see, especially the ones who don't shop there, is the mountain of useless junk that gets dropped off, goods that can't be sold, not by any stretch of the imagination. Clothing so worn, so filthy or odorous, so laced with moth balls or mouse droppings, that volunteers literally swoon when they open the bag.

And the thrift store has to pay to have this garbage hauled away to the dump, where it should have been sent in the first place.

I would like to propose an alternative to business as usual, especially since most thrift stores serve a greater mission, one that directly assists their communities.

Offer to purchase a reverse extended warranty. Simply double whatever price the thrift store asks for this item and say very loudly: "A reverse extended warranty, please."

Normally, an extended warranty allows you to purchase a false sense of security, that when your new product fails to function, which often occurs just beyond its official warranty period, you can still have it repaired. Never mind that the extended warranty is just another cheap marketing device, a gimmick to increase the cost of your already inflated price tag. Many warranties today (if you read the small print) also require that you pay the return shipping costs — which often amount to half the price of the product itself.

A reverse warranty, however, is a better deal, at least in the recycled world. It guarantees the thrift store (and the public that shops there) that if you find, for any reason, the product you are purchasing to be defective in any way, you will toss the damn thing in the trash, where it belongs, and not donate it once again out of some sense of misguided altruistic responsibility.

A lady at the checkout counter of one of my favorite thrift stores had her arms full of some very good bargains she'd culled from the racks. I wasn't far away, browsing through the books, listening to the checkout chatter.

"Oh, that's pretty," the cashier cooed as she removed a hanger and examined the price tag.

"Wait!" the customer shouted, "don't ring that one up!" She sounded desperate at first, then she lowered her voice, as if embarrassed. I had to move closer toward the jewelry counter just to overhear what came next.

"Is three dollars too much?" the cashier asked.

"Oh no, the price is fine."

"Then is the sweater torn or stained? Sometimes our volunteers miss things before they put clothing out for sale."

"No, no. It's practically new, but it looks so familiar I'm afraid I might have been the one who donated it."

I can't think of a warranty to cover that, but believe me, it happens. Not too long ago I purchased a book that was touted to be a riveting read. When I sat down at home, I noticed my own signature scrawled at the top of the title page. And I know for a fact that the book wasn't all that interesting.

CHAPTER TWENTY-FIVE

Wranglin'

As I lift a cup of coffee to my lips, it's obvious that I am in the presence of tension, and not the usual soft, frothy, latte-induced tension swelling up in coffee shops all across the West. This is a serious jitter, an espresso buzz that saws the air with gesture and heartfelt fibrillation.

For the moment the rancher stays on his side of the couch, cradling a hot cup of something with both hands; the young woman remains on my left, gnawing speculatively at the toasted edges of a cream cheese bagel.

The man begins to retell a tale he'd told the woman yesterday, so I can hear what prompted their argument. To keep the peace I nod my head, glance back and forth like a spectator at a tennis match.

The story starts with a ride on his favorite gelding along Stoner Mesa. Here he pauses in the narrative to include a flourish about his fondness for his horse and the sweet mountain air, but then the incident unfolds rapidly.

"I heard a commotion in the trees," he says, "not far off from where I was riding, and I reined up to listen. The noise turned into an outright ruckus, so I spurred my pony and arrived at the scene in ten seconds flat."

Next he describes a scene more compelling than any PBS Nature special, an attack from the old world that ripples for a lifetime across the brain like water from a pebble tossed into a still pond.

"As I reached the edge of the trees I spotted a cow elk with her calf standing off to the side, sorta panic-stricken, watching an old mangey coyote pant like the devil. Its long yellow teeth were slick with slobber, and sharp. Next the coyote leapt and pulled the calf down by the neck. I tried intimidating the mongrel by riding closer, but its jaws were fastened to the calf's neck like a vise. Only yelling and swinging my hat like a confounded rodeo clown could persuade that old lop ear to let go and back off."

Me, I'm listening carefully but I'm also watching the young woman begin to smile. She knows how everything turns out. He, too, glances across the couch along the narrow safety afforded by his years and senses the tension easing.

So what happens to the coyote, I want to ask, but to pause at this point in the story would only declare which side I'd defend. I clear my throat, make it sound like a cough, then retreat to my cup of coffee.

Yesterday the young woman had raised the older man's hackles by defending the coyote's natural right to its prey. I think she's right. Natural selection cannot be dismissed, no matter how ugly, unsympathetic, or vicious we make the predator out to be. The coyote is doing its Darwinian best to secure its own link in that great burden called the food chain.

The rancher says he would have shot the coyote without a moment's hesitation had he been riding with his rifle. I can understand that, too. Coyotes aren't famous for discriminating between what belongs to humans and what is officially on the wilderness menu. Baby elk ribs one night, baby beef the next.

The storyteller returns to the calf after the coyote vanishes. "I stepped down from my saddle to look for damage," he says. "The calf didn't get up. It's a young one, barely two weeks old, still speckled with white spots in the matt of its soft hair. So vulnerable it made my heart break. I reached down and lifted it to its feet. The poor little thing let out a squawk so uncanny that my horse – fearless till now – backed away."

Eventually the calf stands. The mother keeps her distance. The man is relieved to be riding with leather gloves, because he knows he'll leave less scent, something the mother mistakes for danger. "That's how animals do," he points out. "It's their way, to distrust what humans touch."

He rides back to the same spot the next day and sees no evidence that the coyote ever returned; it appears as if the calf rejoined its mother and grazed off into the sunset. Which means, from where the rancher's sitting, innocence is redeemed. And from where the woman sits at the opposite side of the couch, hunger gets little relief.

But from my perspective straddling a coffeehouse stool, I see someone young defending the old, and someone old defending the young. As it should be. Trust me.

CHAPTER TWENTY-SIX

Heritage foreclosed

I have half a mind to say nothing about the closure of 13 Arizona state parks, but then the other half of my mind insists that something be said about boarding up the old Riordan Mansion in Flagstaff.

No other mansion in America is quite like it, a sprawling 13,000 square foot pioneer living space where two families huddled, comprised of 40 rooms, designed and built in 1904 in the Arts and Crafts style of architecture, and filled with Gustav Stickley furniture which was new when it arrived, as well as all the amenities that should have made a frontier town like Flagstaff blush. The house was a gift in 1978 from the second generation of Riordans to the city and it has since 1983 been managed by the Arizona state parks system to stand as an historic reminder of what wealth can build in the middle of a burgeoning frontier town.

The reason I'm saying twice as much as I intended about the mansion is that it's really two mansions – a duplex really – nearly identical structures joined by a 1,000 foot common room referred to as "the cabin". Touring it nearly a decade ago, I was fascinated by the image of the mansion as a Freudian blueprint for the two hemispheres of one brain, albeit constructed out of Ponderosa pine. You see, the two half brothers of Dennis Riordan came out West to make their fortunes by managing the older brother's lumber business, and they just happened to marry the two Metz sisters. These couples built and then set up house in complementary quarters, and during their stay, did much for the Flagstaff community when they weren't thinking about lumber all day or sawing logs in their sleep.

It's really something to see, this mansion of rustic logs and volcanic stone. Or rather, it was something to see, furnished and restored with all the innovative paraphernalia of the era, like hot and cold running water, electric heat, and a refrigerator. There was even an early model of a telephone. Now it's closed. Mice are the only touring mammals, because the place was axed one more time, on February 22nd, due to budget shortfalls. The oversight board voted unanimously to cut its funding and nobody shouted "timber".

It's one more fatality in this ailing economy, because here's the thing: The admission price to see our heritage is skyrocketing. Arizona state parks increased every park fee, in several cases by as much as 100%. They probably consider it justified, but if the parks are suffering financially, what makes them think the people who visit their parks are doing any better? The former $6 admission to tour the Riordian was fantastic, especially when compared to the overpriced tour packages required by other historic homes like Frank Lloyd Wright's Falling Water House ($18), the William Randolph Hearst Castle ($24), and even a national treasure like Thomas Jefferson's Monticello ($31). Knock knock. Who's there? Nobody.

But there's one more tragedy in the making. Closing down outdoor recreational areas like Red Rocks State Park near Sedona or Tonto Natural Bridge near Payson is not the same as shuttering a hundred year old mansion. The living trees and shrubs can nurture themselves without human interference, and they may even be better for a lack of tourist traffic, but the logs, roofs, walls, and floors of the Riordan Mansion can't simply be dusted and left to fend for themselves. Profit should not have been the only priority in deciding to close the Riordian Mansion. The integrity of such an old log building requires a level of vigilance that can't be ignored and leaving it open would have gone a long way in sustaining and maintaining its delicate history.

My only consolation in this matter is that if the closure becomes permanent, the mansion legally reverts to the family. And with a little luck, maybe the Riordian ancestors will turn half of it into a water park and the other half into a shopping mall. We don't have enough of those now, do we?

CHAPTER TWENTY-SEVEN

The line of aridity

$\mathcal{E}$very other day each summer, for four sloppy hours, my wife and I turn on the irrigation pump and drag garden hoses around like unwieldy snakes, so that the land surrounding our house doesn't dry up and blow away. It's a chore nobody covets, but the work results in a shade of green that we consider envious. Located as we are, west of the 100th meridian where irrigation takes over for rainfall and the skies are not cloudy all day, we whistle a slightly different tune from those people who pucker up from all the moisture they need. Certainly, there are scattered exceptions, but overall westerners have a drier sense of humor, purchase a liberal supply of skincare products, and are more likely to be superstitious about opening (or even owning) umbrellas.

The 100th meridian is a geographical departure point, known informally as the line of aridity, bearing no relation what-so-ever to any brand of underarm deodorant. When people sweat west of the 100th meridian, they're usually wondering if it's likely to ever rain again. They're worried about lightning bolts sparking against the tinder of national forests. They're measuring the depth of snowpack in the mountains while skiers are obliviously perspiring. In the West, sweat has consequences.

As a child born and raised in the land of 10,000 lakes and 5,000 fish, I knew water to be as plentiful as the air. My childish dream was to one day live beside a river. I distinctly remember not choosing a lake, because lakes reminded me too much of bathtubs. When I moved out west, I got my wish, more or less. My house is situated on a tributary of the Montezuma Valley Irrigation company's network of rivers that supply water to farmers and ranchers. Okay, they're not rivers per se. Technically, they're called canals, just another way westerners have coerced the rain into falling where it's needed.

Yep, I'm talking about canals. Kayakers and whitewater rafters are probably disappointed. People who fly fish are more than likely casting about for a different article to read. There'll be no raging rapids, no monstrous boulders sticking out of the water like ravenous stone teeth. No, just a few flat truths about my placid river.

In addition to the drinking water that flows from our tap, my wife and I are lucky enough to own a miniscule portion of the rain and snow that falls in the mountains: Five shares of it, to be specific. Or to be even more specific, that's 5/80ths of a cubic foot per second. Irrigation companies distribute water in shares, and it's an odd word for a parcel of water – a share – because westerners don't really want to share as little as they can of what they legally own when it comes to water. Aside from natural evaporation and the wildlife that comes down to steal a drink, all the water in an irrigation canal is spoken for. Try taking some that doesn't belong to you and you might get shot. Plenty of old-timers know stories of murder and mayhem, all prompted by a few scoundrels (and not necessarily all Californians) who were loose with somebody else's allocated water.

Venetian culture romanticizes its canals with comfy gondolas and Pavarati boatman who sing their hearts out for the sake of a few tourist dollars. I'm just happy about the tenacity of my canal, which reaches all the way to Towaoc, for even the mighty Colorado River doesn't have what it takes to make it to the ocean anymore. Enough water for the West is a tall order, and no matter how we supposedly share it, somebody at the bar isn't going to get a drink. Most of us know that a dry town is traditionally one where alcohol isn't available, but when it comes to water there is no such thing as a dry town, because without water there's no town at all.

Perhaps my favorite image of both hope and hopelessness for the future of living west of the 100th meridian is an expedition of children with buckets and poles that always strolls past our house, heading to the canal for a morning of fishing. Little do they know that MVI releases three times a year a chemical similar to copper sulfate into the canal in a successful but expensive attempt to reduce algae growth and discourage the existence of fish. Still, the kids walk down the county road with the picture of fish jumping in their minds, tugging on their lines, expecting, like so many people moving to the West, that just by heading out they'll find what they are looking for.

CHAPTER TWENTY-EIGHT

The ego has landed

If you ever want to see the epitome of what is called a "starter castle," then I recommend you visit close to the real thing, the Hearst Castle on the California coast.

This once-upon-a-time bastion of privilege conquered by the California State Park system sits on a bluff overlooking the Pacific Ocean. Close to a million people bought tour tickets last year, and I confess that I was one of them — twice.

From this same bluff where I stared down at the ocean this past summer, the young William Randolph Hearst romanticized his childhood after numerous camping trips with his family. Though Hearst lived a majority of each year in New York City where he eventually directed his huge newspaper empire, and though he traveled extensively during his 88 years, Hearst remained devoted to his family bluff at San

Simeon. Like so many people with disposable incomes, who are inspired by some element of lofty elegance in the natural world, he transformed a perfectly noble promontory into a flagship to his ego. In other words, he reduced what he loved into one more mansion with a good view.

I mention this not because I have any vendetta against the Hearst family, but rather, because too often when I glance up from the highway toward one of our more local majestic vistas, my view is truncated by another palatial home perched on the skyline like a pseudo-Hearst Castle. Hearst has been dead now for over half a century, but his legacy of insecurity and conspicuous consumption endures.

I would be less than honest if I didn't admit that the allure of a prominent vista has plagued me since I was a child, drawing me to the edges of high things where I could feel the exhilaration of the earth rushing up to meet me while my mother would clutch at her heart, praying I wouldn't – with my rather clumsy gait – trip and rush down to meet the hard dirt. Maybe it's the same instinct that accounts for the mountain sheep staging its life from high in the Rockies, or those big birds that pirouette so close to the sun on extended wings. I mean, I can sympathize with the impulse to soar from any summit, to capture in your heart for a few moments a breathtaking view. It's another thing entirely to carve a half-mile driveway to that summit while dragging a half million dollars of construction expenses behind you.

On the walk-through of Hearst Castle we had the chance to ogle half a dozen priceless ancient tapestries, along with other booty purchased by Hearst and shipped to America. At one point a member of our tour snapped a photo with his forbidden "flash" option turned on. The guide curtly responded with a warning, and we moved along in single-file, keeping our hands to ourselves while our eyes scurried like mice across the floor and up the walls. At the end of our guided maze we were loaded back into a cage with wheels and we descended to those heights more often reserved for mere mortals.

I started worrying after returning home from California, because vistas are what the West is all about. If it weren't for declared wilderness and acres of publicly owned land, the mini-castle movement could potentially buy up every inspirational panorama under the self-serving philosophy that if a mountain exists and nobody has built a house near the top of it, then it's impossible to hear anyone sigh. I know at first that sounds ridiculous, but California residents are already battling in court to establish public-ocean access where private homeowners have built a wall of mansions between the land and the beaches. Let's not forget, though we think of our lives here in the West as high and dry, that a tide of human flesh is forever rising, lapping closer and closer at our foothills.

I should warn all those people out there with their homes teetering on the pinnacle of reason that one day as I'm driving along, I just might be stopping. They needn't worry that I'll be admonishing anyone for claiming the skyline as his or her own property, and I won't be monkey-wrenching any delicate artery that keeps electricity, water, telephone, Direct TV pulsing into their mountain havens.

No, the knock on the door will be a timid one, coming from a man who just wants to look around, to take the 50-cent tour, to see first-hand how close to the edge we need to get just to see the difference between awesome and awful.

section three

Polishing Off the Apple

CHAPTER TWENTY-NINE

The landfill poet

As any election season draws near, I once again want to announce my candidacy, to put my own name forward, to nominate myself for a prestigious title: Poet Laureate of the Montezuma County Landfill.

The truth of the matter is this: There are only three driveways located closer to the landfill gates than my own, and none of these neighbors writes poetry. I think I'm the most qualified for the position.

During the entire history of literature I don't think there has ever been a landfill poet. And no wonder. At the landfill, Americans spend their energy getting rid of things, not memorializing them. Poetry, however, is written to capture intense moments in words and, like nuclear waste, preserve them for what feels like a million years. Somebody responsible needs to be in charge. Poetry's half-life demands an attentive ear.

I know people will ask, "What's the point of designating a landfill poet?" I would answer this fair question by encouraging non-readers to pick up a book of poetry once in awhile, not just the trash. My campaign motto is this: Choose what thinks, not what stinks.

As a grassroots advocate, I would remedy our county's confusion concerning poetic expression. LaPlata County residents only respect the word meter, because it's enforced when it comes to parking tickets, not Wordsworth or Keats. I want something more for Montezuma County, to be able to recognize beauty, even at the point of absurdity.

Another question to surface during my nomination process no doubt will have to do with the awkwardness of associating poetry with a landfill. Why do I want to bring poetry, a form of literature with a reputation for grace and sophistication, into a collision with trash compacting and sewage? And once again, my reply is simple: Poetry must be recognized as language distilled, condensed, trimmed, and uncluttered – composted, for lack of a better word. What better place to celebrate poetry's power than at the location where our lives are compounded with the dust?

Of course, not everyone has positive feelings about poetry. Voters have despaired because some poets bury their poetic sensibilities so deeply, the point of what they've written can't be excavated. I promise, if I receive this nomination, to make poetry an uplifting experience. If it's legal and I can manage it without having to pay an additional dumping fee, I'll distribute copies of local handpicked poems at the landfill gate, or have them printed on the back of landfill receipts. I say, it's about time we feel illumination, not just elimination.

Now that I've gone public, I suppose there'll be a

barge full of candidates vying for my position. So be it. There's nothing better for politics than a healthy debate over ideals, philosophies, and ethics. What better way to challenge anyone than a public forum for those who would dare to sit quietly in a room full of poets.

Let me close with a small contribution from my apocrypha, a ditty that prompted me to consider running for this position. Readers, if you can hold in your minds the rhythms of the William Tell Overture, you will hear not just a poem but an anthem.

To the dump,
To the dump,
To the dump dump dump,

In my truck,
In my truck,
In my truck truck truck,

With my junk,
With my junk,
With my junk junk junk,

And I pray
It won't take all day.

CHAPTER THIRTY

Nothing up my sleeve

Immediately after Valentine's Day strikes at the heart, thoughts turn toward Easter, those sweet memories of hunting marshmallow chicks lurking in the cellophane grass. For a time we believed that rabbits laid eggs, or that the big chocolate bunny would be just fine with ears and feet nibbled down to stumps, didn't we.

When one of my students asked if she could present a speech on domesticating rabbits for food, I guardedly approved the topic. I was afraid she'd put everyone to sleep by reading a warren report. I reminded her that even rabbits get bored; she smiled and told me not to worry.

On the day of her speech she pulled from her deep jacket pockets – by the scruff of their soft necks – two baby bunnies. The audience was suddenly all ears; the air filled with oohs and aahs. But then the moment passed.

"Let me hold one," a voice shouted. "No, I called it first," a contrary student replied. I turned off my stopwatch. I set my grading sheet aside. The rabbits slid from desktop to desktop, and I waited, by now the only person in the room remotely interested in hearing what this teenager wanted to say.

While the rabbits made the rounds, my young speech student explained how piercingly these cuddly animals could bite and scream. She talked a little bashfully about the rate at which rabbits reproduce, but her confidence returned when she offered a few vivid details concerning the extra whack bunnies require at the back of the head, just in case they started squirming while the cook removes their skin. The class paid no attention; they could only hear with their eyes.

Her tour de force consisted of a piece of advice, that children would eat rabbit if their parents could convince them it was chicken. A few faces in the class quizzically glanced up with an odd expression that bordered on realization. They looked at the bunnies, they looked at the speaker, and they partially understood what had until now still been fuzzy.

Once upon a time a national news story reported on a teacher who wanted to supplement her students' book learning by showing them how a calf the class had raised became a side of beef. The school district required parent permission slips before the students could accompany their teacher to the packing plant. Some of the parents balked at the thought of sending innocence into such a dark corner of reality. I can sympathize. There are times when we desperately hope nobody is paying attention.

My speaker finished, sat down, and everyone seemed comfortably readjusted to the notion that words in a school setting have very little to do with life. I scanned the desktops to see if the bunnies had left any jellybeans behind – they hadn't. And to my relief, nobody got bit. We politely applauded and the two fluffy visual aids made their way back to the speaker's deep pockets where I asked that they stay for the remainder of class.

The class exhaled a collective sigh of disappointment.

I insisted on quiet and called for the next speaker. Except for whispers and a few furtive glances in my direction, I noticed that nobody could keep their eyes from wandering over to the rabbit speaker's mysterious pockets. A new student took center stage and spoke on a topic none of us can any longer remember, probably doing his or her best to keep from twitching and blushing a deep shade of pink. Three more lifeless speeches followed, and then the opportunity to work as a professional entertainer came back to me.

My fear is that the public wants teachers to pull a rabbit out of a hat every day, for every child, in every public school across America. That would be nice, but sadly, the lessons that strengthen our bones are not as sweet as candy. It's difficult to compare reading, writing, and math to any of the basic food groups. The challenge of educating today's youth continues to make me feel inadequate. And I would probably be a better teacher if I could just believe the one piece of advice my speaker took to heart on the day the rabbits invaded my classroom, that so much of life would go down much better if it tasted a little more like chicken.

CHAPTER THIRTY-ONE

A gram of truth

While the students darkened the bubbles on the survey forms with their number two lead pencils, I sat in my chair at the front of the classroom and surveyed the class. They had been assigned the task of completing a drug questionnaire, an annual statistical portrait of our youth that provides funding for our school district's Student Assistance Program.

They groaned when I handed out the booklet, but they went right to work, relieved to know that I had no interest in dispensing a grade for their answers. My instructions required that I make available a large manila envelope so students could place their completed surveys inside it; the last student finished was to seal the results.

Ten minutes into the survey, one student's hand shot into the air. "Yes?" I responded. "What's Derbisol?" the student inquired. I had no idea, though it sounded an awful lot like a young mother's solution to relieve an infant's teething pain.

I asked for the page number the student was working on and picked up an extra copy of the survey. The item in question read, Have you ever used Derbisol? Then it asked, How often? Clearly, here was a drug I knew nothing about. "Sorry," I said, "I can't help you on this one but if you ever find out, I'd like to know." The student smiled and continued filling in the bubbles.

I finished the day with this new drug stuck in my thoughts. Apparently, enough young people came in contact with such a substance – perhaps even on a daily basis – to include it on a major survey. While I knew everything I needed to know about Byron, Keats and Shelley, Keroauc, Ginsberg and Ferlinghetti, I had no idea where Derbisol crept into the cultural picture. In all likelihood I had unwittingly crossed that dangerous line called middle age and begun my inevitable trot toward the shady lane that leads out to the pasture.

Derbisol? It sounded like it had the makings of a big-time pharmaceutical, a prescription drug gone under the counter. The next day I stopped by to pick the brain of our resident "Health" expert, a man who, if he hadn't heard something about it, at least knew how to find out.

Unfortunately, he had no more idea than I did, but having taken the opportunity to ask one of his students who appeared to know his science, he guessed that Derbisol served as an ingredient in many video and computer cleaning solutions. "Ah," I said, "then it works like an inhalant?" He carefully sucked in his breath: "Perhaps," the health guy said, "perhaps."

The next day while working in the library with my class, I headed for the spot where the medical reference books are shelved. I pulled a few volumes down, flipped to the index, and scanned for the word, Derbisol. Once again, the drug eluded me. I went over to the dictionary, the one that might give me a hernia if I were to lift it off its pedestal. Still no Derbisol.

I was beginning to suspect Derbisol of being a hallucinogen, one that vanished without any trace when the authorities started looking for it. The librarian noticed my puzzled expression and asked if she could help. I told her my problem, wondered if Derbisol could be a nickname, like Lucy In the Sky With Diamonds. She promised to check the Internet.

Later she handed me a copy of an article. "So, how do they take the stuff?" I queried. "They take it with a grain of salt," was all she'd say.

It seems that in designing drug surveys, writers often include an item or two to check the reliability of their respondents' answers. The writers invent drugs like Derbisol. The drug is a fake. The survey writers made it up. But in some tested groups, results indicated that as many as 5.6% of the respondents reported using these non-existent drugs. Clearly, here's an awkward high, especially when compared to the slim 3.6% who reported using heroin. That makes Derbisol a far more popular drug because, well, mainly it's cheaper.

And I guess honesty is a substance that we abuse. From the peasant on up to the president, little lies define who we are. We tend to alter reality just enough to get by. The collectors of drug survey data disagree with each other over the practice of throwing out results that reveal lies, claiming that maybe heavy drug users don't remember names of the drugs they have taken. Yeah, and maybe the other fictional drug, Menotropin, helps women forget about menopause.

I know parents all across this country worry about influences their children will encounter when they enter the public schools, especially the high schools. Here's abiding proof for me that one overwhelming influence is still as prevalent today as it was back when I went to school: The desire to appear no different than anyone else. It's not that drug abuse is not a problem to take seriously, but when I see a student raise his or her hand in the future and ask, "What is Derbisol?" I'm just going to say, "It's worse than heroin," and that's the truth.

CHAPTER THIRTY-TWO

Fortunes of the real war

Finishing second in the Olympics gets you silver.
Finishing second in politics gets you oblivion.
–Richard M. Nixon

These days there's not much to be said for the integrity of the American presidency, so when I say I admire something about Richard Nixon, it's likely I won't get a lot of respect either. He may have been a liar, a crook, and possibly even cheated on his mother's income taxes, but recently I've been forced to reassess the man and he's turned out to be slightly better than I thought, at least in my books.

You see, I hunt for used books in thrift stores, books that have some resalable value to book dealers, collectors, and antiquarians. Nearly five years ago I found a copy of Richard M. Nixon's The Real War in a cardboard box on the floor of a

Farmington thrift store. I never read it and truthfully, nothing about finding the book made me want to read it. What interested me was the signature on the title page: Richard Nixon.

At first I doubted, like the war itself, that it could be real. The book was in fine condition, practically untouched, probably unread. I paid a dollar for it and headed back to Cortez with my little piece of history. At home I compared Nixon's handwriting with facsimiles on other documents he'd signed and realized the signature was authentic. I thought, Wow, this book must be worth some money! I was elated – not my usual reaction at seeing Richard Nixon's name in print.

But the elation didn't last long. I took The Real War around to several book dealers in Flagstaff and Durango and the best offer I could get was $15.00 cash or $25.00 trade. One bookseller even told me he wasn't interested in the book.

"You must be kidding," I stammered. "The book has Richard Nixon's signature in it. Richard Milhous Nixon. The 37th president of this country!"

"Sorry, there's no interest in Richard Nixon anymore," the dealer replied.

Like Nixon, I resigned myself to a philosophy of wait-and-see. Each time I picked up the book in its cardboard slipcase I imagined I was shaking hands with a former President. The handshake felt stiff and lacked any warmth – exactly how I suspected Nixon's handshake would have felt – but for me, the book embodied the man.

I stored it in a closet where the light of day rarely entered. Poetic justice for a man who kept us in the dark for so many years, but also darkly tragic for a public figure who spent 27 years in politics, failing and then succeeding, making comeback after comeback, finally achieving the highest office of the land. When Nixon died in 1994 I marveled at my foresight, for I had already laid his book to rest, and I'd almost forgotten I owned it.

Then, with a rustle of newsprint, I heard Deepthroat croak in the media. In my mind, Nixon resurfaced. I pulled the book out just to look at it, and I swear the silver edges winked at me. I'd met a new dealer in Mancos who dabbled in selling books on ebay – an electronic consortium for public opinion expressed not in words but in dollars and cents. He agreed to list the book, but cautioned me not to expect too much. He advised setting the starting bid at a mere $9 and then wait the required seven days.

On the second day of the listing the bid rocketed up to $16.99, but interest fizzled again. No new bidders for another day. My only consolation was that if the book sold so cheaply, at least the buyer would be forced to pay shipping costs. As is the case with electronic auctions, nothing much happened until the final day of bidding – actually, the final hour. Then the bidding got furious: $62.05, $101.25, $121.08, and eventually, in the last minute, $152.51, plus shipping.

I had Nixon to thank. He'd not only signed the book, but he'd managed a comeback from the grave.

CHAPTER THIRTY-THREE

A page turner

We were shopping at a rather upscale thrift store on the way to Glenwood Springs. Normally we don't buy much when prices rival what we'd pay at Wal-Mart, but it's fun to look at other people's junk and laugh about what some ebay savvy volunteer thinks its worth. Our usual strategy to uncover the best thrift store bargains is for Pam to scout out the housewares, appliances, nick-knacks, the clothing racks (both women's and men's), furniture, tools, crafts, electrical devices, music and videos, textiles and linens, seasonal bargain racks, and of course, the glass cases where you have to ask to touch any particular item. For my part I go straight to the book section. In about a half hour we meet (usually in the book section) to confer about what we found that deserves a second look.

"They have a ceramic humidifier for the top of our stove, but they want $30.00." A heavy sigh follows the quoting of price.

"Oh, go ahead and buy it," I reply. "I found a book of love poems that I'm taking home."

Then I hold the book out for her to see, open to the page where I discovered a $50.00 bill masquerading as a bookmark. A smile spreads across her face. Once again, we found a good deal, a book for a buck with 49 additional reasons to love poetry, but it's Pam's expression that's priceless.

A person who reads can probably explain how ideas get into books, but I doubt anyone knows how the other stuff gets in there. Mostly it's forgotten memorabilia, pressed blossoms and four leaf clovers, stubs from concerts and airline tickets. All of it tells a story the author never intended, one we may never fully understand, but it's great fun speculating.

Once at a Durango thrift shop I had picked up a copy of Yoshikazu Shirakawa's Himalayas, one of those big coffee table books, lush with full page color photos of nothing other than the Himalayas. The price was almost right at three dollars, but since the book wasn't a first edition, I doubted I could trade it off to a book dealer for much more than my cost. I decided to let it go, so I set the book back on the floor and leaned it against a bookcase, which is when I noticed the sign hanging from a shelf: All books half price. I snatched the book back up. In the short minute it remained unclaimed, two shoppers had already made their way across the room to hover near me, no doubt coveting my mountains.

At home that evening I opened the book and flipped through it, admiring many aerial shots of the world's highest peaks. To my surprise, some of the colorplates unfolded to create double-page panoramas. The effect was extraordinary, and I'd have easily paid the full three dollars for the experience, but what I found next more than doubled the effect.

Hidden in three of the six foldable pages was a cache of two dollar bills, thirteen of them, all in mint condition. Someone must have thought of the book as a hidden safe. The advantage of using a book this way is that you don't have to remember a complicated combination, but you do have to remember which book is the safe.

Immediately I wondered if the two dollar bills were valuable, like winning lottery tickets waiting to be claimed. I hadn't seen a two dollar bill in a decade, but an internet search revealed it to be more of a novelty item, a denomination any bank can provide for the price of, roughly, two dollars.

Some of the best finds, however, are not necessarily cash. Old books have the panache to reveal a few idiosyncrasies about their previous owners. Inside the front cover of a 1941 edition of Short Stories for Study, edited by – I had to look twice – Raymond Short, a student of the University of Buffalo's 1945 graduating class signed his name, George J. T. Stubblebine. On the back cover, under the heading of "Fooey," he listed three compositions he'd been assigned – proof for me that students were no more passionate about writing in 1945 than they are today.

I've uncovered author's signatures on title pages, including Richard Nixon's, and I have an envelope with a matching sheet of stationery from a luxury hotel. The Potter, formerly of Santa Barbara, California, opened in 1903. As a major American beach resort, the hotel could house up to 1,000 guests, some of them wealthy enough to arrive in their private railroad cars. My stationery has a pre-printed date line that reads "190___." Folded inside it, flat as the paper itself, is a 100 year old pressed flower. The hotel burned down in 1923; my flower may be all survives.

Of everything I've found, though – and I've cracked more than a few spines in my time – one discovery stands paramount to all the others. It was a story, simply the best I've ever read. I could tell you where I found it but it's more interesting if you look for yourself.

Chapter Thirty-four

Life as a PERAsite

A retired educator with whom I often take my midmorning coffee break has been at the retirement business longer than me. Since 1983 he has been living off his investment, which has been generous enough to include the price of coffee. The way I figure it, I'll need to purchase and consume over 5,460 cups to catch up with him.

One morning while we were sipping in the sun he announced he was living a parasitic existence. It sounded unhealthy and I wanted to ask him if he had a tapeworm or some kind of mite, but how do you tactfully ask that kind of question? Then I noticed he was still smiling, so like the un-schooled sucker I was, I asked: "What exactly do you mean?"

"I'm collecting a retirement check each month that exceeds the amount of money I contributed to the fund," he replied. "I'm living the life of a parasite."

Biologically, he was right, because a parasite is an organism that lives on another organism and benefits by deriving nutrients at the host's expense, but technically, he was slightly inaccurate. As a former educator, he's actually a PERAsite, one that's attached to the Public Employee Retirement Association, a Colorado fund that functions much like social security for many of the state's public workers. PERA had been investing his money like a poker player for 28 years, anteing up his contributions every working year to be dealt into the longevity game.

My friend has been retired for 23 years. Last year he received a letter from the PERA people informing him that his beneficiary would not benefit from his death. He already knew that. But they felt obliged to inform him that his investment had expired before he did. Naturally, those are not the words the PERA people used in the letter, but the tables and charts explained everything.

PERA, like many retirement strategies in these lean economic times, is in financial trouble, though the Colorado legislature recently approved a plan to increase PERA's solvency by reducing cost of living increases to existing retirees, stepping up contributions from employers and employees, and pushing back the age of retirement for those who recently joined the ranks. In other words, by the time I'm dead PERA hopes to be profitable again.

I got to thinking about my retiree, who was thinking about himself as a parasite, and I wanted to explain how the insurance and retirement investment industries function as the real parasites. On my way to retirement my health insurance premium increased for 27 years and I redeemed a small percentage of what I paid in. I know, I'm lucky. I've insured my vehicles for 40 years and claimed virtually nothing. Lucky again. My houses have been protected against most kinds of disaster, and I'm still lucky my life has been so claim free.

Still, it bugs me anyone could make such a generous man think of himself a parasite. The insurance industry is the real creepy crawly thing that profits by juggling an actuary table of risks against the hazards of living and like a casino, more often than not, the corporation wins.

I'm happy my retired friend is alive beyond his calculated window for survival. I hope we all live as long, so that we can reclaim our invested interest. As for me, I'm thinking longevity has something to do with coffee. Black. Just lift that cup up to your lips and sip that sucker dry.

CHAPTER THIRTY-FIVE

The department of corrections

I put my uniform on, attach the ring of keys to my belt, then slip my photo ID lanyard over my head. I don't wear a gun, and truthfully I wouldn't want one, even if I was authorized to carry a weapon. Apparently – at least based on the reactions I get while making my rounds – I can do as much damage with a red pen. You see, I am a high school English teacher and I've worked in the department of corrections for the past 25 years. When I pass compositions back to my students, they sigh like inmates, cover their faces, and weep for the crimes they've committed. Sadly, only a few of them change their ways, and so the same errors are repeated, over and over, generation after generation.

I don't know why the details – commas, spelling, subject/verb agreement, passive voice, and the use of apostrophes – are so difficult to manage. You'd think with all the published books surrounding us, suitable role models would lead to a healthier, less grammar-challenged society. But in my State of the Union speech concerning our struggle to teach English in the public school classroom, I'd have to report the war is not going as well as planned. We may even be losing the battle, partly due to the insurgents who believe text messaging represents a higher moral ground. To me it's an efficiency that reduces communication into a series of technological evolutionary grunts.

And yes, I'm aware I sound too much like my parents when they were complaining that Rock & Roll music was just garbage coming out of the radio. I really do understand that language has always changed and will always change. If the word Sparrowfart amounted to a Middle English way to say "Lovely dawn" then what's the chance Hey will go down in history as an expression of tenderness? I mean, duh, like, when did anything ever remain the same?

Still, like my parents who never owned a cell phone, I too am an anachronism in an age when most people in my cell block own one. You'd think they'd been sentenced to serving adolescence in solitary confinement, compensating for their perceived loneliness by talking almost to themselves, and constantly, sometimes even conversing with a friend further down the hallway – a friend they'll probably be sitting beside in five minutes when the next class begins. If the urge to communicate is so intense, you'd think it would be impossible to stop young people from writing letters or personal opinion essays. Yeah, right: LOL.

Sitting in lockup with an official like me staring you down, trying to convince you that learning to write correctly is important must be like visiting the zoo and ending up with the gorilla feeding you bananas. It's not appealing, because most of the inmates I work with can't get past the notion that the bananas are supposed to be for the gorilla. To express a thought in its simplest form is beautiful, but to dwell in the thought, to develop entire paragraphs exploring it, well, that's another sentence altogether. I mean, CU L8R – I G2G is not exactly what Shakespeare's Polonius meant when he said, "brevity is the soul of wit."

As a correctional monitor, I'm supposed to teach the sentence, not administer it. With an adequate budget for teaching materials, I could supply every student in my classroom with a personal cell phone. Their rehabilitation would begin by requiring they write vanity license plates, thousands of them, just like prisoners used to produce in the service of the society into which they'd eventually be released. They'll be restricted, of course, to using only six letters. Soon that will get boring.

Then I'll move to bumper stickers, fully formed witticisms running no more than the length of a twelve inch ruler. From bumper stickers I'll move to obituaries, and from obits to billboards. For the entire writing curriculum my charges will furiously push their buttons, or I'll be pushing theirs. No photographs or sound bytes. No paper, pens and pencils, or flat panel computer screens. Just words, plain old English language, fully formed and edited on a cell phone's display, all perfectly thought out before anyone ever presses the send button – to me.

By the time I get to fully loaded paragraphs, it's likely the cell phone will be seen as a tedious instructional device. If nothing else, they'll understand how their freedom will be expedited by creating a string of beautiful sentences and not just serving them. And if that doesn't work, at least they'll be sick to death of text messaging on a cell phone by the time they're released for good behavior.

CHAPTER THIRTY-SIX

The last summer vacation

I know how tragic it sounds, the last of anything. But this ending for me has a beginning, one that needs some explaining. It's actually an end wrapped in a beginning, like a Mobius strip, a loop that drives you crazy searching for the point where it all starts.

Over two decades of work as an English teacher in Southwestern Colorado and a major financial investment in the Public Employee Retirement Association (PERA) has led me to believe I have something to live for – namely, a return on my investment!

When I attended my first PERA meeting, a forum offered by the organization to clarify benefits and time lines for teachers contemplating retirement, three other people attended. I was the oldest person in the room. The presenter, a 30-year-old woman, was articulate and attractive. She knew enough about retirement strategies and benefits to be mistaken for a 60-year-old if I simply closed my eyes, but I barely blinked. I thought, How difficult to be so young and know so much about being old.

When I first started teaching, I was 28. I swore I'd never stay in a job I hated just to cash in on the retirement package. Luckily, a career in teaching has never been lucrative in stock portfolios. I stayed in teaching because I thrived on the interaction with young people, and I loved language so much I wanted to convince a few of them that words are what we are made of, as a society, as a species. Language is blood, which is not a metaphor. We actually wake up wagging our tongues.

The organizers of the retirement info meeting served cookies and lemonade, as if a few treats would distract us from remembering we were spending a few hours of our summer cramming at retirement school. I felt sorry for the woman who prepared a PowerPoint presentation but couldn't get the projector to function. If she ever wanted a change of careers, from presenter to classroom teacher, she had all the inexperience it took. So the five of us had to huddle around the laptop computer screen like we were at a campfire, and she told us the story of retirement.

I've nurtured another passion, this one for over 30 years: Learning how to write. And yes, I'm still learning. I'm not sure how to explain it to others, but after 30 years I'm certain this career called writing has me by the throat. My investment in it, however, had better be calculated in hours, not dollars. If I worked out my total time spent and weighed it against the money I've earned as a writer, would anyone take me seriously? Still, it's not like I could stop myself from writing, and it's impossible for anyone like me to ever retire from such a career.

Teachers are an envied bunch when it comes to their summer vacations. Over the past 27 years I've spent a good part of my "time off" studying – taking classes, paying tuition, earning teacher license re-certification credits, and an advanced degree. Still, I've enjoyed the summers. And now that it's summer again, or technically, the last summer, I want to take a deep breath and remember, in words, what I can't quite say when people ask: What are you going to do now that you've retired?

I'm going to wake up to the sound of the sun rising, not the sound of bells and school buses.

I'm going to hum in the bathroom while sitting on the toilet.

I'm going to stack paragraphs like the people in Iowa stacked sandbags before the flood.

I'm going to see the dentist without applying for sick leave.

I'm going to read a book and not consider how I would teach it.

I'm going to cut the grass in the middle of the week.

I'm going to eat when I'm hungry.

I'm going to play cribbage with my friends, a penny a point.

I'm going to contradict myself, because I contain multitudes.

I'm going to be a farmer and grow old.

I'm going to open the mail when it arrives.

I'm going to mentor my insecurities.

Yes, it's summer vacation, not really the last one, but the one that lasts.

section four

Wreck-
creation

CHAPTER THIRTY-SEVEN

Ripple

We're paddling down the Animas when my river pal, Al, points toward a rock sticking out of the water like the cusp of a giant molar. The river's full force rushes around it and I nod my head, mentally marking the danger, but he still keeps pointing.

I look again and I finally see the wreck: A broken aluminum canoe pinned against the rock's upstream side. Al shouts that it has been there for a couple weeks, that some-body got swamped and probably abandoned it, a barter with the river in exchange for a life.

We back-paddle to slow our drift, scrutinizing this badge of another paddler's folly. Al, a seasoned river runner, has seen it before and so for him it's just a Post-It note to re-mind him that litter need not be confined to parks. For me, though, it's a billboard analogous to those warnings on the highway that say "Buckle Up!"

But as is the case with rivers, the current insists we move along. When we finally put ashore downstream, I can't get the image of that broken canoe out of my head. My uneasiness circles and shapes itself into words.

"Let's stop by that wreckage on our way back to town."

"What for?" Al asks. Then he shrugs, tosses his life jacket into the back of the truck, and we begin to secure his canoe to the rack.

It hadn't occurred to me before I made my request that spoken words name the wish we harbor, and secretly I longed to wrestle the wreck loose from its perch and portage it back to my garage at the edge of the painted desert, my ancient sea in Cortez. You see, living all these years beside an irrigation ditch doesn't necessarily mean that I have no ambition for rivers.

As we pack Al's gear away and prepare to shuttle back upstream, I tell Al a nostalgic story about a time in Minnesota when I rented a canoe just to sit and reflect on the unbroken surface of a lake. On the drive back up river, I'm talking about the past but I can tell he's considering the future while he listens to my meander. As he looks at me he calculates the risk. In a world that's fair to river runners we'd all own canoes and kayaks and we wouldn't have to beg our friends to take us paddling. It's also clear from the wrinkle on his brow that he doesn't really want to stop by the wreck on our way home, though his eyes seem to say, Well, at least it isn't the Titanic. Then he shrugs his shoulders again as he pulls off the pavement and says with his heart, Why not.

I hop out of the truck before he can silence the engine and get the winch out of the toolbox. While I attach one end of the steel cable to a sturdy tree, Al unties his canoe from the truck and carries it down to the water, a short distance above the snag. Then he fastens his life jacket and helmet. I offer to be the one attempting to lasso the renegade canoe, but my inexperience at navigating fast water is obvious.

"Nah," says Al, "I used to rustle trout on a fish farm."

Who could argue with that.

Al attaches a short piece of rope to the hook on the winch cable, pulls the lead aboard, and pushes off. To my amazement he catches the bow of the broken canoe on his first pass. He paddles ashore below the snag in time to watch me grit my teeth as the winch's steel cable stiffens. I crank away, fearing that the canoe's aluminum will rip, but miraculously the river eases its grip and the boat slips free. I feel like Ernest Hemingway having hooked that fabled big one, and when I glance behind me, Al is all smiles.

After we haul the wreckage to shore, we examine our booty. Suddenly it all seems useless. Both bow and stern have retained their narrowed shape, but they're pointing in nearly the same direction. The middle has sagged and the frame appears twisted. There are jagged gaps in the aluminum where the river's teeth ripped through.

"It's too small, maybe we should throw it back," I offer.

"Nah, we can pound those sides back into shape, and I have just the thing to patch those rips."

With the remainder of the day and the first part of the night, we reshape the wreck into a semblance of its former self. The middle never comes out right, but because this is my first canoe every flaw melts away.

"You know," Al says, "it's just a fishing canoe, never intended to run a river like the one we pulled it from."

"Yeah, I know."

"And it's never going to maneuver quite right, and it's heavier than you want to lift by yourself, and it's going to be a bitch getting it tied to the roof of your car."

"Yeah, I know that too."

* * * * *

On the way home I stopped at a liquor store to purchase a bottle of something I might break over her bow for a christening. Port sounded poetic but in the end I settled for a bottle of Ripple, a cheap wine popular with college kids and derelicts. It's not that I didn't value the experience of salvaging a broken canoe. No, it was the twist-off aluminum cap that convinced me not everything has to be priceless to be perfect.

CHAPTER THIRTY-EIGHT

Paddling for pleasure and pain

A Keowee is a kayak, so to speak, built for two. Unlike a tandem bicycle, though, when you stop paddling you can't brake or even slow down, especially if you are riding a rapids. The Keowee I refer to might never have belonged to me in the first place if I hadn't managed to talk the owners into selling it right when they were planning on donating it to be used as a salad bar centerpiece for a local riverfront restaurant. The marketing vision went like this: Fill the empty space in the kayak with ice and within that portable glacier nestle some salad accouterments. A real showpiece. Free advertising and all the salad you can eat.

An experienced kayaker would know better than to try navigating a salad bar through dangerous rocks and rapids, but I knew more about side dishes than kayaking back then, and hungered more for the latter.

The owners recommended kayak lessons in a swimming pool: Learn to roll, to bail, to paddle and steer, to actually read a river so as to avoid getting confused by the plot, which tended to move rapidly in one direction. I nodded, thought "what a good idea," then my wife and I went straight to the first river we could find and pretended it was a swimming pool.

We studied the routine of preparation: I found it a little embarrassing at being forced to put on a skirt before climbing into a kayak, then using it to close both of us into a chamber not so different from sealing a Tupperware container. My level of skill I borrowed from my experience with canoes on Minnesota lakes. As we climbed in the boat, my wife volunteered to paddle in the front. Her reasoning went like this: If he drowns I want to be the first to know.

Many kayakers provide great photo opportunities along the Animas, masterfully weaving through the gates, muscling their way up channels and down chutes, making the entire business of kayaking appear a lot simpler than it actually is. The first time we tried to defy what the river current demanded, though, our kayak tipped, filled quickly with cold river water, and we were chasing our gear down the river instead of shooting any rapids. We began learning our lessons in the school of hard rocks.

Our first expedition placed us in the spring runoff about ten miles above the town of Dolores. We engineered our own shuttle by chaining my old bicycle to a tree in town, then driving north, unloading our gear, and attempting to keep our feet dry. Before we'd traveled hardly a mile down river, we ended up with more than wet feet when once again we capsized. The river must have been hungry, for it swallowed my glasses and used one of our brand new fifty-dollar paddles for a toothpick, putting an awkward twist into my efforts at learning to navigate a kayak.

Our second expedition placed us back on the Animas River about the same distance above the town of Durango. The first few miles of the trip went well; we enjoyed a fairly quiet and peaceful float, and even handled a few adventurous rapids. This led us to quickly gain a false sense of confidence that would prove to be dangerous.

As we neared the end of our trip we saw the Main Avenue Bridge in the distance, and like a game of pinball we wondered which of the three slots would set off the most bells and lights. Ultimately, that choice was not actually ours to make, for the current forced us into an enormous log that had been jammed against one of the cement abutments. Our kayak slammed into the tangle, tipping us into the water and pinning us against the wall, where the river blasted us like the thrust of a jet engine.

Chance managed to pluck me loose. On my way out, I grabbed my wife by her helmet, and we were suddenly free to follow the rest of the debris down river. The lesson was simple: The river doesn't give a damn what it swallows.

Our final expedition took us to the San Juan River, an overnight, permitted trip applied for about a year in advance. In the interim we had lost a teaching colleague and friend, Michael Miller, to the cold-blooded waters of the Animas. He was a seasoned river-runner, yet one whom the river refused to forgive for making perhaps just a single mistake. Our kayaking innocence had begun to wear thin. Next to Michael, we were Laurel and Hardy, fools caught in the slapstick of our efforts, surviving, but laughably. We might have canceled our trip down the San Juan except that in our family, to waste money constitutes a sin greater than wasting our lives. Unfortunately we had already paid our fees.

The water temperature in the San Juan River in June made getting wet feel like sitting in a Jacuzzi compared with our previous immersions, which was a good thing, because the mosquitoes and flies at the Sand Island put-in were so fierce we jumped into the water to rid ourselves of their incessant irritation.

Packing, we realized we had brought far more than we needed; every inch of space in the kayak was crammed with too much plastic-wrapped gear. If our kayak were to go over and get away from us, we'd be stranded, our overwrought plans once again tweaked and this time floating rapidly toward Lake Powell. At the time, though, these threats didn't occur to us. Once we got on the water, a leisurely pace and an empty river left us blissfully alone in our ignorance. With the exception, that is, of two motorized rafts and eleven Boy Scouts that appeared out of nowhere after my wife and I had stripped naked and stood helplessly on a sandbar washing the day's grit out of our shorts.

The rapids – Four Mile, Eight Mile, and Ledge – provided more than enough excitement for us; we walked around them. Or, as W.C. Fields might have it: We drew out our trusty sneakers, hacked our way through a wall of brown water, dragging our kayak behind us. We bathed in the warm moonlight that evening, then camped on a ledge, the river soothing our tired souls with its song all night long.

The next morning at Mexican Hat, we loaded our boat onto our truck, gave five stranded foreign travelers a lift to Cortez, and retired our gear. For good. It turned out that, for us, the river's song wasn't worth the risk required just to get to hear it.

In the fall we had sold our boat to a couple that had "always wanted to try kayaking." We recommended first taking lessons in a pool and warned them of the dangers. They smiled and waved as they drove away, excited, no doubt, at the idea of conquering a river or two.

Chapter Thirty-nine

Shifting gears

After riding for 25 years atop my old English 10-speed – with skinny steel wheels, tape-wrapped handlebars – plus an additional five years with the same 10-speed functioning strictly as a sanctuary for spiders – I finally bought one of those fancy, 21-speed mountain bikes.

When I got the new bike home – they don't call them "bicycles" anymore – and leaned it against the wall in my garage – where did the kickstand go? – I sat and pondered this new world.

Hanging upside-down by two hooks in the ceiling, my old bike stared at me reproachfully, cobwebs glistening. If spokes could speak, they might have intoned, "Grasshopper, are you ashamed of your teacher?" In fact, I was. Ease had become my religion: Quick-release hubs, gel-foam seats, rapid-fire shifting, aluminum frame – this was a technological stew simmered by corporate executives and served up as a modern bicycle. Bike, I mean.

At our local bike shop the owner can talk your ear off if what you want is information about riding. When I asked him how expensive a new bike could run, he pointed toward a muddy specimen leaning against the counter and said, "That one runs about $4,000."

I looked at him again and swallowed hard. If a support group for naive mountain bikers exists out there, I had blurted out the words that qualify me for membership: "You must be kidding." He was not. I then toured the shop, trying to make sense of all the nouveau bike stuff.

A few labels showed me I was in the province of an entirely new culture. One pair of shorts reasoned, "This features the capillary action and the fast moisture-transfer capabilities of microsensor and ultrasensor fabric." A simply jersey postulated, "We designed an innovative 50 cm zipper that eliminates the bulky look of exposed zipper teeth." Clearly, this was high-tech wear with a jargon all its own.

Back in my old bicycling days, I never had to worry about what to wear. If the weather felt cool, I wore a jacket. If the sun was out, I wore my cutoffs. If there was thunder and lightning, I pedaled like hell and felt lucky to get home with just a muddy stripe up my back. I had no image to defend; I was simply a guy who went out for a ride.

Riding back then brought to mind the image of John Wayne, cowboy boots, blue jeans, and cowboy hats; no Ultra-suedefleecechamois shorts with Hydrofil Lycra liners.

It's all changed. I stood in the bike shop and stared into the vortex of complexity, wondering if those olden times were somehow better. Was it more genuine when I borrowed my mother's clothespins to attach baseball cards along the fenders that would flap against the spokes as I rode? To think today of how many collectible baseball card fortunes I squandered back then makes my head buzz.

No, it wasn't better, just different, and now it was past time to join the times. So I chose a specialized brand. It cost as much as my first car. As I gingerly led it out of the store, I could envision the entire line of mountain bike equipment that yearned to follow me out to the street: A roof carrier for transporting my bike into the mountains, thorn-resistant inner tubes to reduce the hassle of flats, a CO_2 air pump for emergencies, some better pedals and biking shoes, insulated water bottles, a light-weight indestructible helmet, gloves with the fingers amputated at the first knuckle, mirrors for assessing the traffic, lights, "panniers," as bike baskets are called, maybe even a kickstand, and not least, a pair of pricey little bike pants with a padded bottom.

In the true spirit of the new century, what had modestly started as a simple desire to adapt to the modern world wanted to bloat into a major investment. I could have gone right back inside with my credit card and joined the legions of cyclists who take their equipment oh-so seriously. Instead, I stuffed my shiny new machine into the trunk and cinched it down with good 'ol bungey cords and headed for home. Perhaps I am still cheap.

That was last week. What I haven't done yet is go out for a ride. So today, I rode. But rather than head for the miles of rugged Western mountains or canyon trails, I initiated my new bike by putting on my jeans and boots and riding it slowly a half-mile straight to the county dump. There my bike and I paused before those enormous steel gates and gazed into that final place where all new things eventually rest. The ordeal was chastening, but I have to confess that the ride seemed effortless.

CHAPTER FORTY

The scooter blues

wish I knew why Harley riders stare straight through me when I'm coming down the street on my scooter from the opposite direction.

Sadly, I'm beginning to suspect American motorcyclists of subscribing to a caste system in which Harley-Davidsons occupy the top tier, followed by the Euro-touro blends, the bullet bikes, dirt bikes, and finally the dung of motorized two wheeled transportation, the scooter.

I own a scooter. Americans are buying and riding more scooters. Do we have to organize our own rally just to get a little respect?

It may be that a manifesto tooled into leather and nailed to a dealership door could make our case for a new age on the streets. Not everyone who chooses to ride a scooter is a wimp. Clearly, not everyone who rides a Harley is a rugged individual. I've seen the ladies with blue hair driving their Buicks and believe me, it takes guts to scoot around on our public roads with only 49ccs under our seats.

I'm proud of my scooter comrades for staying alert, remaining cautious and sucking up less gasoline. It's time the big bikes realized they're representing the Hummers and SUVs of the motorcycle world.

If I could market a scooter look – an outfit, say, that screams "take a ride on the mild side" – maybe stereotypes would shatter and the thundering chrome classes would meet us with open arms. Unfortunately, uniforms don't appeal to those efficient souls who ride scooters.

Most of us follow the fashion model dictated by common sense: If it's cool, we dress warmly; if it's warm, we wear something cool; if it's wet, we try to stay out of the rain. Leather, chains, fringed vests, beards, braids and tattoos amount to clutter, and really, there's not enough room on a scooter. Trademark insignias and corporate belonging do little to motivate the modest scootee.

I'm not sure if it's a matter of economics or just sour grapes. In many Western states scooters with engines under 50ccs need not pay for registration, plates or insurance. They can even park on the sidewalks. If I were a big bike, I'd be upset, but there's no need to take it out on the little guys. Let's be role models for each other and try to relax: We won't say anything about 12 bikes lined up in two parking spaces if you'll just disregard our wimpy-looking shopping baskets.

Being ignored as a bipedal without pedals only makes matters worse. The scooter rider already feels invisible at the traffic light, but here's the most embarrassing part. I've arrived at intersections early in the morning when no traffic is forthcoming, especially from side streets. I pull up to the crosswalk where a dozing traffic signal should get some sense of my presence, but nothing happens. The light stays red for me, green for the rest of humanity. I could sit a full five minutes wrapped in my invisibility cloak, waiting for the signal to change, waiting for another vehicle to pull up. Once, I even put my scooter up on its center stand and jogged over to push the pedestrian crosswalk button.

Lately, I've taken to simply looking both ways for traffic and scooting across the intersection regardless of what the light tells me to do. Hey, what I'm doing amounts to a blatant disregard for authority – just like any good Harley rider.

section five

Day Trips

CHAPTER FORTY-ONE

Day use abuse

If you enjoy getting away from the house, feeling refreshed by an hour or so spent in more natural surroundings, and unloading your burdens onto a picnic table, then you may want to be cautious when you go to the woods. Nothing is so wrong with the picnic tables themselves that their use should be discontinued. No exploited nation manufactures them for just a few pennies a day, and they aren't made of sacred wood from endangered forests.

The problem arises when you attempt to perform the picnic function at an actual picnic table on much of the public land administered by the Forest Service. Get yourself situated, open a bag of potato chips, and just like Yogi Bear and his infamous sidekick, Booboo, the park patrol appears. But instead of trying to make off with your picnic basket, they'll ask you to pay a picnicker's fee, better known as the Recreational Access Tax (RAT).

What's wrong with paying for a picnic table? Well, in my opinion, it's really not enough. I would be more inclined to pay the fee if upon making a series of, say, 10 payments the Forest Service would mount a brass plaque to the table with my name on it.

I don't know why the Forest Service hasn't started assessing daily viewing fees for standing near a scenic overlook, or for simply sucking in that clean Western air, thick with a priceless pine-scented fragrance that's probably imported all the way from … California?

I mean, there are so many missed opportunities for raising revenue on our public lands besides this policy of picking on picnickers that I'm surprised the person in charge of determining policy for the administration of public lands hasn't been accused of being thicker than wicker.

One complaint from park visitors stems from some misguided public impression that they already pay taxes for public lands, so why should they, in essence, be taxed again with daily use fees? If I was the person in charge, I'd answer this complaint by pointing out how little money public lands receive compared to the U.S. Military, and if America wants to be a superpower when it comes to operating one of the hugest bureaucratic infrastructures associated with wilderness, why, then people better be ready to sacrifice a few more dollars. Our woodsy reputation is on the line. I'd say, America: Exploit it or leave it. Naturally, I'd say all this while smiling, nodding, and maintaining an even voice with a well-modulated feeling tone. After all, let's not forget that wilderness bureaucrats are professionals, not simply habitat police.

Seriously, though, I think it's somewhat ludicrous to ask for a picnic table fee while failing to consider the secondary needs of the picnickers, as if a firmly mounted picnic table somehow fulfilled the park caretakers' responsibility. Where, for instance, are the salt and pepper shakers? And without napkin holders, any breeze scatters litter all over the park. You'd think for the cost of a day use fee a few hand-painted rocks could be made available to picnickers for use as paperweights. And whatever happened to the traditional red and white-checkered tablecloth, or the water jug, or those pointy sticks we used to hold over the flames to blacken hot dogs and set marshmallows on fire? Maybe the public would be willing to pay more if they felt they weren't being charged for doing all the planning themselves.

Better yet, why not introduce an "Adopt a Table" program? It would be in the interest of bigger budgets and better revenues if we could break down the average mentality of thinking of a picnic as an impromptu excursion, a quickly planned and playfully executed outing where people grab some food and get together for spontaneous laughter and good times.

Rather, if we could recast this national pastime in the American mind as a lifetime commitment to the natural world, an event that is anticipated before the childbearing years and brought to fruition as the new family matures, then we could transform the typical "picnic" into a fine dining experience. We could even add a sense of exclusivity by establishing a star rating system and arranging for reservations.

I can already hear the afternoon diners scrambling for their cell phones: "Excuse me, we'd like a spot near that enormous tree with the pointy needles that overlooks the lake, please." The maitre d' would reply, "Naturally, and would you like your dirt with or without ants?"

CHAPTER FORTY-TWO

The Moab melt

The story actually started in a diner best left unnamed, in Moab, Utah, where I ordered what sounded like a tempting plate of local cuisine: An open-faced roast beef platter which the menu described as "smothered in green chili and melted cheddar cheese." What the waitress brought to my table was a lukewarm roast beef sandwich on a slice of Wonder bread covered in a cheesy, yellowish gravy. The green specks must have been – I hope they were – chilies, because I ate them.

But before I tell you how this sandwich found its way – albeit in an even less appetizing way – into some of the most gorgeous scenery imaginable, picture the desert canyon country on a late October weekend. Turquoise skies and ample sun, temperatures out in the rock world over 90 degrees. My wife, Pam, and I had journeyed to this spot in Utah, determined to camp for the weekend along the Colorado River, to hike some trails we'd heard tales about. These ambitions were sponsored in part by the loan of an old river rat's bible, a book titled Utah's Favorite Hiking Trails authored by David Day. Our friend championed Day's guide as the "best" book on the Utah canyon country he'd ever found. He was right about the book, although, I'd also have enjoyed some guidance on where to stop for lunch. Never mind that the author also failed to mention the aesthetics of outfitting one's self for hanging out in a recreational mecca like Moab, such as how to stay inconspicuous without wearing lycra, how to hold your head high without pedaling a mountain bike, or which style of hydration pack to tote up the trail. I silently thanked the fashion gods no one was around when I took our water supply out of the truck by its plastic milk jug handle.

But back to the diner. While the waitress removed the nearly luminous leftovers from our table, my wife and I made plans to tackle the trail to Fisher Towers. David Day's book offers an intriguing description of the formations: "About a dozen of the strange monoliths stand near the Colorado River... grouped together like petrified skyscrapers from some prehistoric city. The residents of this weird metropolis are an endless collection of goblins and gargoyles frozen in the canyon walls beneath the towers."

It sounded like a scene lifted from Tolkien and the prospect of visiting this "other" city seemed endlessly more fascinating than scouting Moab's tourist shops. Fortunately, Day's book also includes clear maps and directions to every trail, so we entreated no wizards for help; we had no trouble visualizing where we wanted to go and actually arrived at the Fisher Towers picnic area.

We probably ought to have started the hike earlier. Though the sun was still intense, I always forget how much heat rocks can absorb, and I started the hike with a trickle of sweat slipping toward the nape of my neck before I'd even left the parking area. We acclimated ourselves to the necessity of spotting rock cairns as we climbed along the trail, which look loosely like tiny mounds of scat that a rock had shat. I use the word "trail" loosely here because much of it traverses solid rock and no matter how much traffic has trodden the stone before us, the path stays invisible. It's easy to wander off the trail and get lost, and only by searching out these tiny mounds of stones set out by park officials to guide hikers did we reassure ourselves we were heading in the right direction.

After less than a half hour, I realized I missed a cairn somewhere along the way and we were forced to retrace our tracks. I wished I'd saved a few crumbs from my sandwich to drop along the way, because it was likely they'd have remained untouched – the wildlife being scarce and probably more discriminating about what they put into their mouths than me.

The guidebook claimed the hike would last about two and a half hours, round trip, so I thought we'd have ample time to get – as Bilbo Baggins would say – there and back again, but no guidebook can account for the time it takes to get lost, then find the way back to the trail, then get lost again. I am famous for getting caught up in some detail of the scenery and following it toward some sort of conclusion. When I'm merely daydreaming in my office chair I stay pretty much in the same place, but when my feet are forced to digress along with my brain, well, I end up in unexpected places. After about 45 minutes of this kind of leadership, Pam kindly suggested that she take the point and I follow. I am happy to report she regularly glanced behind her at intervals just to see if I was still there. I am a little easier to spot than a cairn.

By the time long shadows began folding themselves into the rocky terrain, my stomach started grumbling and I started worrying. Day's book suggests that photographers arrive at the farthest ridge about a half hour before sunset for a spectacular view of the Towers "when the low western sun inflames the spires' reddish hue." Sounds a little like hell, and I couldn't imagine a 90 minute return trip to the parking area in the dark. Well, actually, I could imagine the return trip, and that was the problem. I saw myself sprawled on my back with several broken bones at the bottom of one of those less majestic overlooks we had passed. And truth be told, that sandwich I scarfed down for lunch had begun to gnaw a small hole in my guts.

So, we headed back.

We saw no human spiders dangling from ropes in this popular climbing area. We passed no other people except for a couple we met heading back toward their car during the first 20 minutes of our hike. We made it back to the parking lot just in time and while Pam sat on the hood of the truck to "ooh" and "ahh" at sunset's light show, I sat in the portable toilet doing a little of the same.

CHAPTER FORTY-THREE

The writing
on the wall

We watched the steady stream of tourists snake its way toward Spruce Tree House, the only Anasazi cliff dwelling at Mesa Verde where the federal agency allowed visitors to guide themselves.

It had been single file since leaving the museum, so we heaved a collective sigh. Petroglyph Trail, which runs 1 ½ miles through the trees along the base of a cliff, took us out of the mainstream. As we moved along we savored the quiet, knowing how brief our isolation would be in a national park that attracts more than 500,000 visitors per year. Sure enough, coming around the first bend in the trail, we encountered two red-faced preteens.

I stood aside and asked, "How were the petroglyphs?" One of the young girls stopped to face me with an unaccountable mixture of adolescent angst and disgust in her eyes. "We never got there, and, like, it's over 5 miles!" Another 500 yards up the trail a middle-aged man made his way toward us. In the 95-degree heat his face glowed pink, a fine contrast with his silver-gray beard. He looked as if he might be wise.

"How were the petroglyphs?" I repeated. He stopped to catch his breath. "It's got to take over three hours to reach them, somewhere alongside marker number 24, and over the next rise is only marker 7," he wheezed. "Years of experience on the Mojave Desert taught me that I'd be a fool to hike all that way without water, so I'm turning back."

After he left, my companions stared at me. "I swear the map shows it's only a mile and a half to the petroglyphs and a mile and a half back," my brother said. We hiked nearly a mile without talking, passing through caches of shade, stepping into brilliant patches of sunlight where we stopped to stare into a sagebrush canyon below us that radiated heat.

I expected to encounter more hikers, but we met no one else. A half-million visitors a year, and today it appeared as if only six of us managed to step off the asphalt, and only three of the six wanted to reach the end of trail, just to see the writing on the wall. Wonderful.

I know it's selfish, egotistical, narcissistic and arrogant of me to believe this, but we need more places in our national parks designed not to prohibit, but to seriously discourage most people. We need to plant more poison ivy, more poison oak. Import mosquitoes. Post warnings about wolves and mountain lions.

We need more risks, fewer snack shops and absolutely no souvenirs made in foreign countries. We need maps without the notation, "You are here."

Then my Catholic upbringing started a fire down in

the soles of my boots, and I felt guilty. It must be wrong to wish that Americans had more difficulty participating in the experience of our national parks. And it must be unsympathetic to add another pound of worry onto the backs of the overweight, or to take away one breath from those toting their oxygen tanks. Was I advocating exclusive access to the national parks for the young and the fit?

Well ... yes and no. Yes to the notion that not all backcountry should accommodate the masses. No to the notion that visitors' IDs should be checked at the gate. Yes to the reality that those who can anticipate and endure the rigors of a primitive trail are the only ones who have business being there. There's something about democracy and freedom that has to leave risk in place.

If the National Park Service had Nepal in its jurisdiction, ought there be a ramp in place to the top of Mount Everest?

I was wrestling with these ideas as we arrived at Marker 20, and I knew that despite the heat and the rocky terrain, we were close to gazing at the petroglyphs. We were lucky, like those who first scratched their symbols on the rock over 800 years ago. Lucky to be alive to see this glimpse of a people's universe.

A week later, I learned from a friend that we were supposed to register with a ranger before hiking down the trail. I thought of sending my brother a stern summons to appear before a wilderness court, but he would plead, like me, that we saw no signs and, even more to the point, we had left no trace. Which is more than we could say for the people who lived there 800 years ago, who wrote their messages on rock walls.

CHAPTER FORTY-FOUR

A spring thing

The Geyser Springs Trail is a part of the San Juan National Forest, percolating not much more than 50 miles from the hot water faucet that fills my bathtub, yet I had ignored this lofty local wonder for nearly two decades of life in the Four Corners.

Once realized, my imagination filled with visions of Old Faithful. My parents took a much younger me to see that legendary billow of steam, the bubbling cauldron, the wooden walkways creeping across the encrusted stone, to marvel at the magnificent sulfurous shower that spouts off every 67 minutes. Wow, I thought, Colorado has its own geyser.

"Let's go see the geyser before we're too geezerly to appreciate it," I urged my wife one evening.

"Too late," she replied, but she agreed to accompany me in case I lost my way back.

We drove early the next morning from Cortez, north on Highway 145, until we reached the West Dolores Road. Pam rode shotgun, guiding me with her modest visitor center brochure. I considered outfitting us with my cache of expedition gear, but then I reconsidered and we took a simple day pack and some water. Sometimes the natural world needs to be approached on its own terms, without all the high tech survival clutter that works mostly to keep back country equipment manufacturers alive. And besides, the hike was short and the directions appeared rather straight forward, with the exception of a warning that prompted me to silently question the simplicity of our expedition: The first part of the trail is on private land and difficult to follow – please do not stray from the path Was it dueling banjos I heard in the distance? And where did that image of a shotgun leveled by an old miner with a trickle of chewing tobacco running down his chin come from?

After several failed attempts at finding the trail, we located a promising fence line and followed it. Just as the directions indicated, it wound behind two private cabins and though we felt a bit like trespassers, we pushed on. Eventually I knew we must have hit pay dirt, because as the trail headed toward the trees I could hear the rush of water.

The brochure's next warning immediately came to mind: Do not cross during high water.

We stood for a moment and admired the river's meander as it snaked through an open meadow. I've always been drawn to the sound of moving water. Instinctively, I bent to touch it but pulled my hand back, as if shocked by the current.

"Cold?" Pam inquired.

I sent back a clacking Morse code message with my

teeth: C---O---L---D, a puff of steam punctuating the spaces between each letter.

Still, we needed to cross. With our boots tied, slung over our shoulders, and our pant legs rolled as high as our calves would allow, we waded into the rushing current. The river quickly kicked at our knees, twisting its glacial muscle against our white, spindly legs. I nearly lost my balance in that first instant of contact, but we steadied each other as best we could and struggled ahead. Our legs immediately ached from the cold, but we managed the distance. On the far bank we sat down to tie our boots back on, and we laughed like a couple penguins as we tried to describe how numb our feet felt.

By now the geyser trail seemed obvious enough, worn by quite a few other feet. It started gradually rising as it headed toward the trees. Several seeps along the way made the ground soggy in places but to accent the dark mud, wildflowers tossed in their spring colors like tiny fireworks all along the way. The quaking aspens quaked with the slightest breeze and though we had been laughing, shouting, and chattering, somehow under the shelter of the trees we both turned silent during the climb, as if the canopy forced our thoughts inward.

My thoughts wandered into the trees, those tall sentinels that measure time by quietly adding another ring for every year of life. I believe that trees live inspired lives, their roots tight to the earth, their limbs loose and filtering the air for light. For me, walking in the woods feels like a kind of worship, as if the very idea of cathedrals originated in the human mind when early architects moved among these slender pillars and stared up at the vaulted sky.

But humans more closely resemble geysers. Most of our lives we bubble and spout, then gratefully turn calm – at least that's what I do if there is some pocket of wilderness I can climb into.

Though the trail spanned a mere mile, the internal distance I traversed seemed vast. If I left the earth and came back again, I don't remember. Moving through the dappled patches of sunlight that filtered through the trees must have induced a trance where my feet functioned separately from my mind, as if on automatic pilot. I didn't trip over any fallen branches, and I steered clear of the ruts where early spring rains had washed the ground away. Or rather, I must have levitated over these hazards, because I don't have any clear memory of what difficulties lay along the path; I only noted them on the trip back down the mountain. On the way up I was elsewhere, circumnavigating the globe, for all I know, caught in deep canyons, listening to waterfalls, stopping in the rainforest where exotic thoughts came to me like so many parrots talking in my head.

Before I realized it, Pam tugged on my sleeve and pointed to an opening in the trees beside a tiny stream. We'd arrived with no one in sight, but we were hardly the first. Perhaps the CCC had been here long ago and cemented stones together to shape a reservoir where the water pooled. We approached the edge where steam rose and mingled with the rank, sulfurous gasses that escaped into the air. A hatch of early flies hovered above the water, interested, no doubt, in what our intentions might be.

"Let's go for a dip," I suggested.

"In that cauldron of scum?"

We stood a while longer, watched the latent broth churn a little as it imitated a lukewarm bowl of split pea soup. Then, as if by a magic spell or a witch's incantation, the water began to boil, furiously, and we stared, convinced that my suggestion to enter the pool had stirred the gods. I bent once again and touched the water.

"82 degrees," I speculated.

Whether I had been extraordinarily persuasive or Pam's feet still felt like chunks of ice, I'll never know for sure, but immediately Pam started taking off her clothes. I have never been the kind of man to stand around fully clothed when a beautiful woman is naked, so I stripped down to nothing, and we both stepped carefully into the water.

We found a tolerable perch on a rock below the surface and settled into the soup, up to our necks. The flies swarmed, the sunlight slipped through a crack in the canopy. I pulled two stems of bracken fern from the bank and set one up-side-down on each of our heads, a silly party hat to shoo the flies away. We laughed, the geyser splashed, we inhaled the sulfurous steam.

I don't claim Geyser Springs has miraculous restorative powers, but it cured me. And what's more remarkable is that I wasn't suffering from anything in particular before I arrived, yet when we left I somehow felt better. Not healthier, but happier. Not invigorated, but strangely cleansed. I had gone down deep, like an underground seep, and come up with an ounce of wonder – that elixir of spring that consecrates new life.

CHAPTER FORTY-FIVE

Clothing is always optional

Though I've never been in it over my head, a good many friends have told me about a spot where the water comes steaming out of the ground, a natural hot tub. Supposedly, the gentleman who owns the property allows bathers to come down a path to the river's edge, use the metal changing shed if they choose to, and then sit in the hot mineral water without paying a cent. It's easy to find, if you know where to look. But always, at the end of each testimonial, someone mentions that clothing is optional. I'm never sure if my friends are challenging me to go there or warning me to stay away.

Now that summer is over and even the blush of fall is beginning to fade, I feel like clothing has become more important to me. I reach out to touch all the fleecy jackets as I walk past them in the store aisles, I check my socks for holes, and a chorus line of hats comes down off the hooks in my closet.

As another friend of mine once remarked when extolling the seasonal change toward cold weather, you can always put more clothing on, but there's a bottom line when you start taking it off.

I don't consider myself a prude when it comes to the human body, but if I sit in any kind of water long enough I start to resemble a prune. Prude. Prune. Little difference in most people's eyes. Just two words whose roots are tangled in the idea of getting old.

A younger woman told me her story about visiting the springs. She said her favorite time to visit the spa was during the middle of winter – better yet, when it's snowing. The thrill for her came from alternating between the heated pool and immersing herself in the cold river. Back and forth, hot and cold. Summer and winter. Yin and yang.

She'd taken her younger son with her once and, of course, they wore swimming suits. After having the place to herself for a while, a strange man came up the path, obviously intent on climbing in. They exchanged civil greetings, at which time he asked her if she knew that clothing was optional. She replied that yes, she knew it, but under the circumstances she'd prefer it if he'd use a suit.

He seemed to have no problem with that until she shifted her attention away from the stranger and back to her child, who was smiling and observing the adults involved in conversation. The next thing she knew the man was stepping over her head to get into the pool and as she glanced up she said, "I was amazed to be staring up at the Liberty Bell."

Though she laughed while she told me the story, at the time she'd gasped and reiterated in a stern, motherly tone: "I said I'd prefer it if you used a suit!" She wasn't going to play

Betsy Ross to any impromptu struggle for independence, and the man swiftly climbed out of the water, dressed, and left in a huff.

This fall I scouted out the location and found it unbelievably beautiful. I am referring, of course, to the natural setting and not to any colorful locals sunk to their necks in frivolity. Now there's a word for dressing up the occasion: Frivolity: (of a person) carefree and superficial. Summer is gone and I miss it. I'm back at work, dressed in my teacher outfit, ready to teach somebody something about language, but my heart's not in it. I'm starting to feel as if the days are a dark sweater I wear to bed, all itchy with schedules and appointments. It would be nice to shed some of that weight, even if the bottom line amounts to my bottom.

Here's good warning for the rest of you. This winter I'm heading for the hot springs. Arrange your schedule if you must, but I'll be there around the solstice, when the year starts turning back toward summer. Naturally, clothing is – and I'll probably end up in hot water for saying this – always optional.

CHAPTER FORTY-SIX

The cow drive

Western highways have something few other parts of the country can boast. I don't mean mountainous vistas or accessible ski slopes. I mean something most other states have removed from their highways but that we tenaciously cling to: Cattle.

Before you get on that proverbial high horse and start snickering, let me explain. You see, I mean, cattle on the highways, not just near them, grazing like a Norman Rockwell picture of ranching life. I mean a herd of 300 or more head heading right down the dotted line in spite of those lifetime-guaranteed deer whistles you mounted to your front bumper. I mean a cattle drive, major cows and cow people carving a cow swath down the middle of a 55 mile-per-hour stretch of country road. I mean full-time cow business, ranchers with-out semi-trucks, steering their livelihood from upper to lower pastures or (depending on the time of year) from the lower to upper ones.

If you've been there, you know what I mean. First there's the pickup truck with a red flag – maybe an old pair of flannels – on a stick, waving to catch your attention. But even before that, attentive local drivers will know what's happening if they're coming up from the rear end of the event. Drivers in Denver, Albuquerque, and Salt Lake City understand the term "brown out" in a slightly different context than we cattle country people. Once these indicators clearly mark the road, there's no avoiding the inevitable. And really, beside those people with desperate appointments to keep who aren't smart enough to own a cellular phone, who would want to?

There's no feeling so close to nature as having your car engulfed and buffeted by a stream of live beef. If you keep the windows closed, your children will hang from the glass like fruit bats, eyes wide, wild with the excitement of the in-your-face experience. It's reality without an ounce of virtual. I've seen children on the curb waving as if they were watching a parade, each horse and rider a celebrity, each cow a moving wonder.

The real interest for me has been in watching the driv-ers' faces as they creep by, for creep they must. Each vehicle becomes just another part of the herd, a techno-cow if you will, joining the slow motion migration. Some expressions behind those windshields are frustrated, spitting inaudible curses against the glass. Others look away nervously, casting cow to cow glances as 1,150 pounds polishes a driver's side door handle.

Once I watched a driver literally shrink out of sight as an excited animal attempted to mount another, less willing mate. I could see the image forming in the driver's head, both animals coming down on her thin metal hood as if it were a cheap motel mattress. Or the rearview mirror glance, all the time suspecting that cattle have no clear preference in their tiny brains for the anatomical differences between a cow and a Ford Taurus. Drivers obliged to adapt themselves to a pace of life that registers below the increments of cruise control express a kaleidoscope of emotion.

Another thing a cattle drive brings out, besides the obvious glimpse of time-held traditions in ranching, is our fastidiousness for cleanliness. My native Minnesotan father, after driving his RV through his first cattle drive in Colorado, rushed to my house and turned on the garden hose so he could wash the pie from his chrome plate. It's a fact: Cows drool. They slobber, they poop, they sweat and moo. They bellow out of their confusion and long for the quiet of a mountain pasture, away from the jerky ways of human beings. And indeed, they should. Cows historically haven't fared well in the contest for the survival of the fastest.

There's a stampede of opinion about how American ranching should keep up with technology; this is where I'll gladly step aside. And not because I don't care. It's just not my spread, not my expertise. But avoid a cattle drive? Not a chance!

Los Angeles continues to stack its freeways and New York digs its subways. If the information highway is going to run right through my living room, moving cattle online would seem to be the next logical step. Thank goodness logic has its limits.

CHAPTER FORTY-SEVEN

A bull market

Here in southwestern Colorado we live in a precarious position. On the open, enchanted land of New Mexico is the White Sands Missile Testing Facility and the Los Alamos Nuclear Laboratory. To the northeast, tunneled one mile below the surface of Cheyenne Mountain, is the NORAD facility – in all likelihood, ground zero in the case of a nuclear attack.

I suspect the Four Corners Monument is posing as an enormous geographic cross hair scratched into the earth for the benefit of those near-sighted terrorists who might take a shot at us and miss. Still, when I can put doomsday worries aside, I take comfort in the knowledge that we are host to a comparable symbol of masculinity and aggression: The Four Corners Bull Test Center, the only high altitude facility in the U. S. of A.

Thank goodness ranchers are a different breed than nuclear scientists. Instead of smashing atoms, they're measuring scrotal circumference. Instead of mapping missile trajectories, they're collecting performance data such as birth, weaning and yearling weights, hip height, pelvic area, and PAD (Pulmonary Arterial Pressure). The meltdown they're worried about is how bad genetics affects their livelihood, especially on mountain ranches. Now if this sounds like a little too much bull for you, take heart: I'm really just a consumer, not a rancher, and if ranchers stay solvent we won't have to eat my words.

It's perfectly poetic that the Bull Test Center, located on 6500 acres near Hesperus, is the original site of a nineteenth century military post, Fort Lewis. Troops and cavalry, commanded to protect native populations from unscrupulous white settlers while protecting white settlers from unscrupulous natives, saw very little to report in the way of action. The government lost interest in the land as a strategic military site and planted seeds to support our agricultural community, an entity that works to feed all of us, regardless of ethnicity.

Bull tests don't provide the only data collected at the San Juan Basin Research Center, but bulls are certainly the business end of the beef industry. A good bull sells for around $1,700 but if a rancher has taken stock of his stock, that bull will sire calves that produce a healthy future. In 1960 an average weaning calf weighed 500 pounds; today a weaning weight of around 650 pounds is the norm. Essentially, the numbers collected at test centers like the one near Hesperus have produced results: More weight, more meat, better profit with fewer cows. Of course, these numbers are considerably less impressive than the cost of keeping a nuclear missile arsenal, but there is more safety in manure than in nuclear waste.

If a rancher is aiming for a reputation, a bull's eye at the performance tests doesn't hurt. Charles Redd, an 1800's Mormon pioneer, had his hands on one of the biggest grazing permits in the area. Besides raising a big Redd family, he bred what came to be renowned as a big Redd bull. The Redd Ranches, near Paradox, have been selling bulls for 50 years, letting 300 bulls loose at a shot, doing nearly half a million dollars worth of business on a single day at the bull pen. Being close to so many bulls must be scary – that's an awful lot of testosterone confined to a small space. A former Monteumza County rancher and teacher told me that often bulls at an auction are sold, sight unseen, over the phone, based on the performance data – based, that is, on the bull's numerical reputation. No longer does a bull have to snort, put its head down, paw the dirt, and see red.

In fact, I wouldn't be surprised if when the gavel comes down it's not just some old rancher waving is credit card in the air, enticing the auctioneer – not the bull – to charge it.

CHAPTER FORTY-EIGHT

Sheep

Once a year in Pamplona, people perch along the narrow Spanish streets to watch some agitated bulls trample some addled brains so bored by life that they offer themselves to be gored. I've never been to Spain, but I've always wondered what prompts that Papa Hemingway urge to seek such a dangerous activity. I know the Four Corners provides ample opportunity for locals to stand by the side of a road and watch a few hundred head of cattle amble past, but it's not really the same. Hemingway might have gone so far as to say, it's just not a MAN thing.

That's why it probably came as a surprise when I asked Pam if she'd travel with me to Bayfield to watch the running of the sheep.

"Sheep?" she asked. "Why do you want to watch sheep?"

"Because I've never been to Pamplona."

Perhaps it was the exotic Spanish trill in my voice when I said the word "Pamplona" that excited her womanly curiosity. Or maybe she just concluded that a trip to Bayfield would be cheaper than a round-trip flight to Spain. Whatever the reason, Pam quickly agreed, and we set out from Cortez to explore our Near East – namely, a small town in LaPlata County.

Sheep trailing for tourists is a relatively new event for Bayfield, though the sheep themselves have been driven down from leased public pastures for nearly a century. Back then it was just dirty work: Today it's an event that organizers hope will churn up a little cultural pay dirt. You see, Bayfield decided to turn a facsimile of the traditional sheep trailing into a festival called Heritage Days, so the children will come to associate sheep with something other than a mantra for inducing sleep.

Pam and I arrived along the crowded business route into town and parked behind a long line of vehicles. We'd shut off the engine at about 9:55 a.m. and the running of the sheep was, according to the flyer, scheduled for 10 a.m. I didn't know anything about the punctuality of sheep, so I hurried Pam along, hoping we wouldn't miss witnessing some young farmer getting blind-sided by a few hundred pounds of wool. Secretly, I'd tucked a large red handkerchief in my pocket just in case I needed to execute a few passes of the matador's cape, strictly, of course, for our own protection. As I said, I'd never been to a sheep trailing, so I didn't know what to expect.

As we approached the corner where Mill Street headed into the Bayfield business district, it was easy to conclude that the big event had not yet happened: People milled about on both sides of the street, or they sat in lawn chairs talking with their neighbors, as if a parade might eventually arrive. We found a grassy spot and sat in the shade, staring back in the direction where everyone's eyes continued to glance. Nobody looked nervous. I sensed no danger. Pam smiled, as if she'd already seen a clown.

In the distance we heard the faint sound of bagpipes, and soon about a half dozen men in traditional Scottish attire marched down the middle of Mill Street, followed closely by a woman costumed as Little Bo-Peep. I had no doubt that sheep would soon appear. A man standing next to me claimed that nearly 1800 little critters ought to be making their debut, but another five minutes passed and the street remained empty. Could it be that the bagpipes frightened the timid creatures? Could it be that the sheep had turned tail and headed back to their BLM pastures?

But the next time I glanced down the street, the intersection teemed with sheep. I grabbed Pam's arm.

"Look. Sheep!" I said. "Are you ready to run?"

"Do you have haggis for brains?" she replied.

As if someone had opened a head gate, a river of dirty wool suddenly filled the street, moving past the crowd in a fluid, almost choreographed undulation. Then, for some unknown reason, the pacesetter decided to leave the pavement and headed for a narrow space between the bumpers of two parked trucks, right into someone's front yard.

Nobody knows exactly why sheep act as they do, but everyone knows that where one goes, the rest will follow. The yard filled rather unexpectedly, like a clogged drain, with sheep. After a few minutes of flock-lock, someone more resolute than the sheep managed to get one of the baffled animals pointed in the right direction. The flock broke free of its quagmire and moved on. In an odd reversal of sheep protocol, the scapegoat followed the herd, and finally a team of horses pranced by, pulling a shepherd's wagon. Then, without missing a beat, the street cleaning machine that had been idling at the intersection with its amber utility light flashing started spinning its big brushes and the event was officially over.

No mangled bodies, no broken bones, not even much sheep dip by the time the sweeper made his run. The festival stood for good, sanitary American fun. The crowd along the sidewalk gathered its belongings and headed off toward the booths set up in the park, which promised a fine celebration of the Bayfield Heritage traditions, but as for the sheep... well, they arrived and departed so quickly that I guess I'd have to say I felt a little disappointed. After the flock vanished, the spectators just trailed along after the crowd, and I couldn't help feeling a little self-conscious, wondering if any of the sheep had doubled back for the chance to stare at us.

CHAPTER FORTY-NINE

The cache can

"Hey, look at this," he whispered.

She hurried over and pressed against him as she tried to see what had gotten him so excited. They'd been rooting around on the shaded hillside through the bushes, rocks, and weeds next to the middle school, but they hadn't discovered what they knew was hidden there. They found empty liquor bottles, cigarette butts, thorns, fast food trash, and the faded remains of somebody's homework from math class.

Then she saw what he'd been pointing at: A condom, still in its package.

"Oh grow up and get a life," she exclaimed, and when she pushed against him, this time he lost his balance and sprawled in the dirt.

Typical antics for 14 year-olds it would seem, but the couple I'm writing about was over 50. I know, because I'm still picking the stickers out of my shorts. I won't identify the woman – she still drinks coffee with me in public – but I will say we eventually found what we'd been looking for: A plastic container, with a screw-on lid, wrapped in camo tape, cleverly hidden beneath a stack of stones on the hillside. We'd almost given up looking, but according to our information 173 other people had managed to find this canister since it was first hidden in 2003. We had her self-respect to maintain, even if mine had already been compromised.

What we found inside the container was standard loot for a geocache. Sometimes called a Stash hunt, geocaching refers to the practice of using location coordinates with a Global Positioning System (GPS) to discover what amounts to buried treasure. Actually, it's not literally buried but cleverly concealed. And it's not bonafide treasure either, but I'm hoping one day to be the first geocacher to appear after a Texas billionaire on a lark leaves the deed to one of his oil wells. If it doesn't happen in my lifetime, at least the hunt will have been exciting.

A cache (pronounced so it sounds like cash, not catch) gets tucked away in some nook or cranny where people like us devote a few good hours of hiking and orienteering to discovering it. Caches can be rediscovered by anyone as long as its integrity hasn't been compromised. Hundreds of caches have been hidden in the Four Corners region. In fact, caches can be tracked down all over the earth. Equipped only with your locality's zipcode, you can see what treasure has been buried near your home by logging on to a geocaching internet site at <geocaching.com>. Of course, you'll need a GPS unit to find it, unless you have, like a compass, an uncanny sense of direction.

The cache we eventually found on the hillside in Flagstaff contained a small logbook where I noted the date of our arrival, and a handful of objects left by other cachers, including a carabiner key chain, a hair barrette, a plastic dinosaur, somebody's pocket change, a worn dollar bill, one necklace, two pens, a couple business cards, and a pair of sunglasses. I kept the sunglasses, because beyond the trees the sky was bright and besides, they were pretty nice shades; I left a handmade ceramic coin with the image of a face etched onto it – something designed in an art studio – to be spent on the next finder's imagination. This may sound like pirating, but I did nothing wrong; I followed the rules for all geocaches: Take something from the cache, Leave something in the cache, Write about it in the logbook. The system works on an honor code and judging from the number of caches we've found intact, honor is more common than previously suspected.

In two months we visited over 15 caches. Some are easy to track down, just off the path, while others are more difficult, because the host has left less information to help. One clue that finds its way into any listing is a set of coordinates. My home, for instance, can be found by orienteering along N 35 degrees, 12.276 feet and W 111 degrees, 39.169 feet. These numbers represent the intersection where I live, not a physical crossing of paved streets but a theoretical crossing of longitude and latitude. I prefer it when intersections stay hypothetical – they're less dangerous to cross.

The coordinates are made possible by 24 Federal satellites designed for military use circling the earth, and it costs me nothing to access their signals except the price of my GPS, plus billions of tax dollars pulled from our pockets to get these satellites built and into orbit. A basic $100 unit can get me within 20 feet of any geocache, as long as trees or roofs aren't blocking the satellite signals and interfering with my GPS's ability to triangulate my position. I imagine the military can do better than 20 feet, but I try to feel compassion for what they're trying to uncover.

Geocaching has taken us to explore wilderness areas in the San Juan National Forest, the Uncompahgre National Forest, and the Coconino National Forest. We've found local caches in and around Cortez, Durango, Flagstaff, Moab, and Telluride, in places dozens of people pass by each day without noticing. You see, we are the couple who appear to have lost something, stumbling and stopping to stare into our hands, getting down on all fours to grope beneath bushes, rocks, and stumps. If you see us, it's best to walk by. Stopping to offer assistance only compounds the mystery. "Thanks," one of us will mumble, "but we just lost our bearings."

Chapter Fifty

A picture is worth, maybe, 25 cents

We'd packed everything in the truck and headed out for a fall trip to the Utah canyon country. Usually I forget some back country necessity, so I pulled out of the driveway with that chronic, partially digested feeling, knowing that a few miles down the highway I'd figure out what I'd forgotten. For 20 miles I ticked each item off my mental checklist: Boots, socks, water bottles, maps, sun hats, binoculars, sunblock, pocket knife, two thick comfy towels, and our slick, new national parks pass.

For the first time in our natural history as a couple, my wife and I coughed up the cash to purchase an annual park pass. No more sneaking into our public lands at midnight after the tollbooth has drawn its shades, and no more sneaking out before sunrise while the tollbooth is still dreaming about collecting revenue. Middle age has turned us into staunch supporters of our national parks, and we carry our shiny plastic card everywhere, just in case we come within fifty miles of a national park entrance where we might quickly pull through the gate, flash our card, and congratulate ourselves on saving another ten bucks.

Thirty miles out of town, with the Dove Creek grain elevator punctuating the horizon like an enormous exclamation point, our 10-minute conversation abruptly ended when Pam announced, "I didn't bring the camera."

Damn, I thought, but I didn't say it.

And then I thought, why am I mentally kicking myself? We rarely bring our camera, no matter where we travel, and when we do we forget to use it. In our household the invention of the camera ranks right up there with a shipment of winter clothing to a nudist colony. I mention clothing because the weather was rather chilly, and we'd left home, wearing shorts and t-shirts, hoping to find a quiet niche in the rocks to pretend it was still summer.

I finally admitted to the windshield by way of a reply to Pam's observation, "Neither did I."

We drove a few more miles in silence, crossing the State line into Utah, and our conversation started up again, each of us trying to account for the discomfort we always feel posing before a camera. I could report the entire conversation, but really, that's the business of a tape recorder, and I didn't have one of those either. Let's just say that both of us distrust the way photos fabricate the illusion of a fixed, unchanging world, and we share a sense of diminution when it comes to photographing the landscape around us. I mean, if a picture is really worth a thousand words, why won't people shut up while flipping through their photo albums?

Our drive ended at Arches National Park, and we

decided to hike in magnificent weather along a primitive trail that wanders away from the main thoroughfare to Landscape Arch. I still think Delicate Arch is my favorite formation in the entire park, but that image, sadly, is chosen to appear in so many brochures, I figured, what's the use of going there. I can get the same view just by visiting any tourist information stop.

Okay, seriously, I know it's not the same thing, but I swear to much of the camera-toting public we encountered on the trail there's not a lot of difference between experiencing the natural world and appearing with some feature of it prominently displayed behind them. The tendency to pose strikes me as a way to avoid the effort of holding the image in the mind, a means of reducing what inspires us to a convenient postcard.

If primitive people were correct in fearing that cameras steal the soul, then perhaps we've stolen nature's soul carte blanche. We have carved it up into Kodak-sized pieces and sold it to America like Hollywood sells its newest film. Yosemite conjures the image of El Capitan with the moon still visible, only the geyser of Yellowstone rises forever in our minds, and Mesa Verde hangs on to its niche with an endless string of nationally syndicated glossies that appeal to our collective, cliff dwelling memory. We rush out to meet these pictures we remember by RV, camper, and bus, pilgrimage to the site of each photographic shrine, and move on to the next. We seek the truth through our viewfinders and if we get the chance to take the picture, we remain convinced that those fools who cry about a vanishing wilderness have merely run out of film.

Like everyone else, we climbed out of the truck with all the others who parked their cars at the trail head to Landscape Arch. Photo naturalists milled about the parking area, near the restrooms, and formed a short line beside the drinking fountain. Some of them were already pointing their cameras, digitally encrypting massive slabs of rock onto their memory cards so they could carry home a few billion tons of sandstone and load it all effortlessly onto their computers. Clearly, the traditionalists were present, too, with incredibly obscene zoom lenses, tripods, filters, and puffy black bags to pack it all down the trail.

Three groups of hikers in two short miles asked us if we'd take their picture. And please, don't get me wrong: We were happy to help out, but our aim to find a quiet spot and soak up the sun became more and more misdirected. Finally we left the main trail, seeking the less populated primitive route, and wouldn't you know it, another couple waited for us to catch up at the next bend.

"Would you mind..." one of them started to ask, but I interrupted by saying, "There's nothing I'd like better than to take your picture." And I smiled. And they smiled. And I pointed and pushed the little blue button that promptly caused the camera to buzz and whir and shrink its telescoped lens back into the camera.

"I think you just turned it off," the nice gentleman observed.

"Yup," I replied.

The sun was climbing toward noon when the heat would radiate from the rocks in a delicious intensity, so we pushed off. To a photographer, noon light means encountering seriously reduced photographic opportunities, when all those artistic shadows slip under the rocks and the world looks, well...overexposed. To us, though, the world was just coming into focus.

section six

Overnight Destinations

CHAPTER FIFTY-ONE

Of mice and me

I never planned to improve upon any kind of mousetrap but for some reason it appears I've done exactly that. This is how it happened: Every year my wife and I spend a few days avoiding the summer heat of western Colorado by camping high up in the White River National Forest. For the past few years we've stayed in a campground administered for the Forest Service by one of those corporations that have secured the campground concession.

Essentially, the corporation posts a guard called a "host," charges twice as much as it ought to cost the public for putting up a tent, and then returns a contracted portion of their earnings to the Forest Service. It's a kind of economic mousetrap set by the federal government to generate revenue without having to hold the cheese.

Anyway, last year as the season simmered toward fall, we got bored with our old habits and habitats, so we decided to try for a new camping spot; we traveled a few more miles down the road to Avalanche Creek where we discovered a rugged gravel road that climbs well above the pavement. Our prospecting instinct told us we'd likely find something more valuable as the quality of the road deteriorated. It might even be like the old days – free.

But as we traveled up Avalanche Creek, signs continued to prevent us from pulling into any impromptu national forest pull-off until we reached the end of the trail – an "official" campground administered by the Thousand Trails Corp. Defeated, we paid our $24 for two nights and found a site along the creek.

We stayed two full days, thrilled to have our routines overthrown by the tyranny of leisure. We felt obligated to eat grapes, nap, read books, go for long hikes and cool our feet in the icy waters along the bank of Avalanche Creek. When it was time to leave, we packed everything – even receipt number 00888053 which we'd filled out and clipped to our site post – and started back down toward the real world, which means basically any direction that heads away from Aspen.

Perhaps our packing was a little too thorough, or our presence in the mountains a little too tempting to the sedate lives that animals must lead. On the way over McClure Pass I turned on the fan motor to circulate some of that fresh mountain air and felt a slight tremor under the dashboard, as if some foreign object had gotten jammed in the blades. I turned up the fan setting, trying to dislodge the obstruction, but the shimmy became a serious shake, so I shut it down, hoping to avoid more damage until I could check things out.

About noon the next day, after a full morning's sunlight preheated the inside of our truck to an oven temperature,

I casually opened one door and knew right away why the fan wasn't working. Opening every window, we drove with our heads hanging outside the truck like a couple of panting dogs, straight to our local mechanic.

I don't know if Toyota understands how enticing their tiny under-the-dashboard compartment for the fan motor might appear to a humble deer mouse, but to the young mechanic who spent nearly an hour on his back working to dislodge and vacuum not one but three stinking little corpses out of their newly acquired lodging without contracting a dreaded respiratory virus, the cleanup was probably memorable.

Next year we'll go back to that spot along Avalanche Creek because, frankly, we don't know any better. And we'll continue to pay the corporation because our public lands are being swallowed whole by a bureaucracy that feeds on campers as if they were just another industry, no different than lumber, mining, grazing or oil.

Next year, with a little luck, the fees will have only doubled and we'll fare better than the three dead mice that had blindly decided on a little family vacation, unaware that the Toyota Corp. would require the ultimate price for unauthorized camping in a wilderness of wires and plastic.

CHAPTER FIFTY-TWO

Nature is just a phone call away

Maybe the hour is too late. Maybe nobody is working the desk, but someone should dial for a wake-up call.

Hopefully the switchboard operator will send it directly to any national or state park employee who is responsible for implementing the 1-800-reservation system used for campers attempting to stay overnight in public campgrounds.

Hopefully a few groggy voices will answer, slightly irritated, wondering why their sleep had to be interrupted for something as silly as a wake-up call when they will swear it must be a mistake.

You see, we should be irritated, too, since our state and national parks have opted to go into the motel business. If you don't believe me, pull into most any state or national campground early on a Tuesday, Wednesday, or Thursday (just before the weekend) and count the number of camping sites already paid for by people who are still at home sleeping at the very moment you are treading on their reserved ground. Don't, by any means, try to put up your tent for the weekend. Some wild-eyed stranger a day or two later will probably inform you that you are camping in his spot.

Recently I pulled into a campground in the White River National Forest near Marble, Colo. A large sign just beyond the pay station declared, "Sites 8 through 38 are managed under the reservation system," though I noticed only seven sites generously set aside for people like me, who attempt camping without any foresight. I thought, for an instant, perhaps I had accidentally ventured into a KOA.

I prepared myself mentally to negotiate a short-term lease as I drove around the circular access road, studying the tiny white plaques clipped to brown posts announcing that every camping site was reserved for either Friday or Saturday through Sunday. Why, this isn't a KOA, I said to myself. This is a Holiday Inn done in a forest motif.

I continued driving along what must have been a dirt-carpeted corridor, sequential posts arranged like numbered motel rooms, expecting a maid to push her cart out from behind a shrub at any moment. Very clever, I thought. Now, where have they hidden the pool?

It's just plain dollars and a lack of sense that allows people to believe campers on public lands are better served by being able to reserve pieces of our wilderness areas as if they were planning to dine out at an expensive restaurant.

Reservations can be booked as much as 90 days in advance, allowing vacationers in theory to spiritually occupy their, say, Fourth of July campsites in early March, even before the spring equinox. This isn't camping. This is a speed-dial telephone race. Have your charge card number ready, though: They don't take personal checks.

How does the Park Service justify pressuring the public into making a plastic charge card promise as a prerequisite to having an outdoor experience? They would say, we campers forced the system on ourselves. So many, many people want to use our parks at the same time that there's literally not enough room for everyone to converge at the same place, without having to turn some of us away. If you recall, two vacationers in Bethlehem had a similar problem, though even they managed to find a spot to pull off the road for a night or two. And it ended up making a better story.

The fact is the Park Service's reservation system caters to those who vacation with itemized itineraries and travel agents, not people intent on spontaneously and creatively exploring and discovering the magnificent natural resources an unfamiliar area has to offer. The Park Service, like American Express, wants to make one thing clear: Get a reservation. Don't leave home without one.

This is wrong. These are public lands, for goodness sakes, not private hotels and motels. If you want a reservation to vacation, call a Howard Johnson's. Towels, ice, and a tiny bar of soap ought to come with the deal.

Maybe as taxpayers we should fund a bill to purchase neon green "Vacancy" and "No Vacancy" signs for our public campgrounds. Maybe we should raise a bigtop over the trees and build a mountain of bleachers, because more than one campground host has quietly told me, "It's a circus out here on the weekends." Or maybe we should install parking meters at each site that curse very loudly when your hour is spent.

Excuse me, is that a Ponderosa Pine I hear ringing?

CHAPTER FIFTY-THREE

Generator X

camped two nights in LaPlata Canyon, early June. Spring runoff was at its peak. The sight and sound of water roiling just 100 feet from where I rested my head had to be exactly what the manufacturers of sound therapy machines were after when they digitalized the soothing nuances of nature and recorded them to be played on portable devices that fit on a bedside table.

I suspect the manufacturer of the portable generator running in the site beside mine was not concerned that the word soothing would never be used to describe its product. Watts, fuel consumption, total weight, peak performance and efficiency had to be its buzz words. And buzz it did, all afternoon, cranking out the power to run my temporary neighbor's second home.

His 36 foot 5th wheel trailer with dark tinted windows and an expandable room sucked power like a sponge. I checked the rig out when nobody was home, paced its length and scouted its license registration. A couple neatly sawed logs were stacked picturesquely beside the fire ring. I supposed they gave the campsite a sort of primitive look, but the image that popped into my head involved roasting marshmallows over a burning generator.

I also checked out the machine, a 7.8 horsepower gas model, scanning it for a kill switch I could flip if it continued to drone. I figured nobody would leave it running all day without at least returning before sunset to shut their power station down.

The first night of my camping expedition, that's exactly what happened. A truck finally pulled in, parked, and somebody promptly turned the generator off, exhibiting a modicum of woodsy etiquette. Park campgrounds everywhere prohibit the use of generators at night while campers try to sleep.

The next day after I returned from my excursion, the same generator rarified the air, and again, nobody home. How rude, I said to the tree beside me, to leave a noisy generator running and not be obliged to listen. Maybe as one gets older, campgrounds start to look more like Comfort Inns.

I am not, however, blind to the advantages of the gas engine. In fact, I had just anguished over the purchase of a mower for my three acres, having spent days looking at electric cordless models. I wanted something small, quiet, and more responsible than a traditional gas mower, but every online forum recommended an electric for cutting up to an acre. My lawn was wily, the kind of green that grows out of control, especially when I spend so many summer days camping.

In the back of my pickup truck sat a reconditioned gas mower. Any moral high ground over my neighbor had been leveled by that purchase.

As dusk approached, I scouted my neighbor's site once more, scrutinizing the generator more closely. Then I had an idea.

When he finally pulled in to shut off his generator, I would climb out of bed and start my new lawnmower. Maybe make a few passes around my campsite, spruce up the grounds around the old spruce trees. Maybe be a good neighbor and offer to cut his. Let the engine idle for a half hour or so between our campsites, break it in properly.

When he actually pulled in and shut down his power plant, he spoiled my plan. I wanted to get out of bed, but the sound of spring runoff rushed through the open window. A breeze stirred the aspen leaves above me. Birds chirped. Even better than silence, the sounds of a primitive campground returned. Powered by nature.

I fell asleep and slept deeply all night. I woke before sunrise and packed up, prepared to head home. I did slam the truck door quite a few times. Unnecessary, really, but not uncalled for.

CHAPTER FIFTY-FOUR

Pardon my intolerance

I don't know if it was proper to make a gift out of something somebody else threw away. It was just a book, a 1945 edition of Emily Post's Etiquette, with its dust jacket more or less intact. I'm a guy who's fond of recycling. I also refused to wrap it before I gave the book to my friend who loves to laugh at the way things used to be.

For 654 packed pages, Emily (or should I say, Mrs. Post) tries to clarify what constitutes proper behavior in a changing world, from "Mrs. Three-in-One Gives a Party" to "Telephoning, Smoking, and Out-In-Company Manners." She notes that the text for her book has been "rewritten...because the problems of modern life demand certain changes in the forms of living." If Mrs. Post could see us now.

Of course, a book like this still might have a place in our time. Awkward and thoughtless behavior still exists, particularly in the rural West. When was the last time a monster truck parked its front tire up on the curb of the sidewalk where you're walking, or you were forced to listen to an RV's generator while snuggled in your sleeping bag beneath a canopy of stars? Would Emily, even by doubling the number of pages, have had sufficient room to say what needs saying about the way we jostle for space on the public lands, particularly on trails shared by hikers, bikers, horses, dogs and the occasional wild animal?

Post-It notes would be more efficient for me, and for other people on the go: An Emily Post-It Guide to Rude Behavior. It's not so much the accumulation of etiquette knowledge that's important; rather, it's the ability to stick what you know in, or literally on, somebody else's face.

The Apprentice, Judge Judy, Don Imus, and Dr. Phil are all symptoms of a societal infection that rages within us: The desire to tell people off in the most public arena possible. Quick access to the right thing to say could be a Post-It plus.

Vehicles, for example, pose us with a new challenge for polite behavior. Emily's advice on car-passenger etiquette might easily be updated in my new Post-It edition with a few of the following sticky notes: Dirt becomes you. My horse trailer looks like your RV.

I scoured the 14-page index to find some reference to outdoor etiquette, but apparently, people's behavior in 1945 was so driven by class that rules for engaging the natural world now feel unearthly. Instead of trying to negotiate an equitable means for motorized and non-motorized enthusiasts to share wilderness trails, Emily points out that shorts are still only "proper for the young and slim," that older women are strongly advised to choose their bathing suits with the word "ample" in mind, and that the thought of bare-toed sandals with evening dresses is "too revolting to mention" (although she does, of course, mention it).

These days, I want to know how to stop someone from talking on a cell phone while standing in a cliff dwelling, and if kicking over trail cairns, trashing restrooms, tagging rock faces or trees in the back country, or tossing cigarette butts out car windows are behaviors society has to put up with. Maybe we need a new public land motto: "Take only memories, leave only sticky notes." I can't control what people wear, but they wear me down with their rude and obnoxious attitudes toward the natural world. If it ever was truly important to treat each other with excruciating respect, then it's doubly important to treat our public lands with an even greater regard.

The book I gave away contains a black and white photo of a uniformed maid, tray balanced in one hand, posing before a partially opened door. It's captioned with this tiny bit of pre-Post-It wisdom: "[The house] may be of no size at all, but its details are perfect, and its bell is answered promptly by a trim maid with a low voice and quiet, courteous manner." Naturally, I was tempted to draw a mustache on her upper lip before giving the book away, but Emily in her long-winded style is unintentionally correct: This mansion made of earth could always use a few more servants.

CHAPTER FIFTY-FIVE

Between a rock

The first time I hiked a trail in canyon country almost 30 years ago, I had never seen a cairn. In Minnesota where I was raised, if anyone planned to use rocks as markers, they'd have painted them white and lined them up along the driveway. I'd like to think I was not the only newcomer to the desert Southwest to be confused by a pile of rocks, but it's possible.

Since then I have hiked many trails and come to appreciate these stacked rocks as a subtle system of canyon turn signals. Most of the time when a hiker comes upon a cairn, the next one is visible in the near distance. This is not, however, the case in deep backcountry. Here a hiker can easily get lost, owing to the way the native rocks used to assemble cairns blend in with the rocks around them, and also to the tendency for the human mind to wander aimlessly while the body trudges along the trail.

My mind, for instance, wanders quite a bit. Once on a hike to Fisher Towers near Moab, I took a wrong turn and nearly ended up stuck on all that slick rock after dark. The guide book called it a "day hike," which meant I should have started in the morning, not in the late afternoon. But how long could it take to walk 4.2 miles? The map estimated walking time at around 2.5 hours, and the book described the location as a "Popular, easy to follow trail."

I missed a cairn about two miles out and wandered at least another mile before realizing the only stacked rocks in the distance were far too large to be cairns. They might have been the monumental structures known as the Fisher Towers, though I never found out. The sun had already dragged huge shadows out from under the rocks, changing the landscape into an alternate reality. By the time I'd made it back to the last cairn I remembered passing, the sun had melted into the horizon. I had no flashlight, no companion, and no sense. Luckily, this time I followed the correct rocks and they took me back to my car, where it represented as a sort of mechanical cairn abandoned in the parking lot, a perfect pile of junk to leave behind just in case park personnel were called to organize a search and rescue.

One other reason I get lost so often is because the desert Southwest has a noteworthy cairn planted in a place not plotted on any map.

When Ed Abbey died, his friends – sworn to secrecy – spirited his body away and buried it illegally on public land somewhere in the canyon country that Abbey loved. When I come upon a healthy pile of rocks in some difficult and inaccessible area, I tell myself, *Don't worry, it's just another cairn erected by thoughtful people to lead me to safety*, but a tiny part of me still walks around it, looking for the skeletal remains of a foot or hand that might be sticking out from between a couple stones. And I say to myself, Ed, if you're under there, just stay put.

Then I turn and hike briskly away in virtually any direction.

CHAPTER FIFTY-SIX

One mile inn

We eased off the pavement, onto a dirt track that twist-ed through a tangle of shrub oak and pinon. We were looking for a place to stay the night, a small pull off if possible, hidden from the road, with just a little patch of shade.

My original plan involved stretching out under the cottonwoods across from Newspaper Rock, but the site had been closed to vagabonds like us due to an ever-present terror threat in canyon country: Flash floods. Enormous boulders that demanded heavy equipment to move appeared like trolls at every access to the clearing, blocking our way. We were be-ing protected. Despite the unusually warm, dry weather, signs unreservedly announced, No Camping.

Oddly, these unfortunate circumstances led to the greatest fortune, because while I know that national forest land is essential for the environment, I also know it's good for a few impromptu pull offs, and in our search for a camping alternative we stumbled across the gem of them all. Just enough space to park, a towering half century old pinon as a sentinel: No garbage, no traffic, no other campers. I consulted my compass and my odometer: Exactly one mile from the national forest boundary.

Pam, of course, elected to name the location, as if she'd been assigned Eve's responsibilities in this faux Eden: One Mile Inn. No towels, no ice machine, no swimming pool, but an inspiring view of an 800 foot scramble into a pristine canyon. The sound of rushing water threaded through a canopy of trees below us. I announced we'd take it, then proceeded to unpack the truck.

While the sun still searched along the horizon for its spot to settle in for the night, I pulled out a book I'd been anxious to open, one I'd recently checked out from our local library: Beyond the National Parks: a Recreation Guide to Public Lands of the West. I opened it but couldn't concentrate on the words, the maps, or the pictures. A wild turkey called repeatedly to its mate from somewhere on the canyon floor. A breeze scraped against the pinon needles above my head and like an old LP record the music was irresistible. What else could I do? I closed the book and allowed my eyes to translate the landscape.

National forests and libraries have more in common than most people realize. Both depend on taxpayer supported operating budgets, and both are charged with the necessity of providing public access. I've never camped overnight in a public library, but the idea of sleeping beside the stacks, as the librarians call them, has a certain appeal.

Libraries and national forests share another characteristic: Both represent the purest spirit of democracy any society could ever dream up. And sadly, both receive inadequate funding, despite their essential missions. No matter where I am in America, national forests and libraries are open to me – that is, while they still possess the means of staying open, but the privatization and corporate management of America continues to make me nervous. Concessionaires already operate in our public campgrounds and national parks. How much longer before my pull off turns into a pull over, with park police checking my National ID to see if I fit the description of Tom Joad. Barnes and Nobles, Amazon, and Alibris, the dot-com bookshops, already manage our information as gatekeepers of the publishing industry. Our heritage will likely be available at cost, plus shipping and handling.

All these thoughts sat propped against a rock, weighing me down, as I looked out over the canyon. Pam swore it would take a hike at daybreak to release me from my dread, so we went to bed. I dreamt of the scramble down through the tumble of scree and talus, toward the invisible and mysterious sound of rushing water. I thought, if nothing else, something magical must be at the bottom of it all.

By sunrise we'd picked a likely trail and headed down the slope, sighting toward a fresh patch of aspen trees. Naturally, the path that appeared simple from the top proved difficult, with impassable slopes ending in impossible drops, and with visions of access turning into dangerous slips and slides. Pam abandoned the gracefulness of scrambling and lowered her center of gravity until her butt slid along the rock surface. It was that steep. I grabbed gravity's hand and lunged like a drunk from ledge to ledge.

When we eventually arrived on the canyon floor, a

torrent of spring runoff forced its way through a thicket of willows, so thick we couldn't see to the other side. Spring was raging. I knew we could go no further, but we'd managed to get down to the water's edge. I felt elated, weightless, panting like a puppy that's just chewed up a tennis shoe.

On our way back to the top we heard a loud, infernal combustion roar from the canyon floor: Motorized engines – 4-wheelers – aggressively making their way along some invisible river trail on the other side of the willows. I looked at Pam, she looked at me. She shrugged her shoulders. Her face was an open book – unpublished, of course – on the subject of public access.

CHAPTER FIFTY-SEVEN

Into the woods

In fifty-five years on this planet, I've only seen two bears in the woods and neither of them doing what bears allegedly do at this location.

The first bear encounter happened during my initial trip to the Boundary Waters wilderness area in northern Minnesota over 30 years ago. I'd talked Pam into a backpacking expedition a good distance away from civilization. We camped by an ice cold stream called the North Brule in early summer. In one week we'd seen a crazy moose stomp through our camp, a vicious weasel chase an ill-fated baby bunny to its long and drawn out death in the brambles beyond our campfire, and as I said, a bear digging through a mound of stumps and leaves.

My other encounter with a bear happened just last fall, while camping with the same woman near the historic ruins of an old mining town, LaPlata City.

Seeing a bear in Southwest Colorado is, I suppose, not unusual, but to go ahead and tell the story about seeing it borders on cliche. I hesitate to even mention it. Anyone would be completely justified to counter with their own tales of bear encounters, each one of them no doubt more spine tingling than mine. I'd say no more, except that I nearly soiled my pants, so I think a few more details are necessary, if for no other reason than to account for the silliest bear encounter in the history of camping.

Our camping spot on the road to Kennebec Pass – though not a formal campground – had an unusual orange flyer stapled to a post when we pulled in. I got out of the truck and walked over to read it. The flyer, printed in bold, black letters, declared "Bears are in the area." For me, it wasn't news. I was aware that bears inhabit the Southwest. They are in the area because they live here. Newspaper accounts have gone so far as to document their dexterity with sliding deck doors and kitchen appliances every year. Bears coexist in our environment, along with deer, elk, mountain lions, coyotes, rabbits, mice, and human beings.

Pam said, "I wonder if we should stay here."

I said, "Don't worry, the forest service just posts these signs to avoid getting sued."

After we'd set up camp, I offered to accompany Pam on one of our a favorite hikes – the trek to visit an official campground toilet. We'd embarked on this excursion dozens of times, and we knew what to expect. Our route took us along the edge of a gravel road, and as is common with hikers who set off for a specific destination, we settled into our stride and fell silent, listening to our own thoughts.

Rule one in bear country: Make noise. Instead, I was

meditating on the question of whether I should have brought some toilet paper.

Last year a record number of nuisance bears had been executed by wildlife management personnel – 59 in Colorado to be specific, by mid-November, with expectations for more executions predicted due to a lack of cold weather and early snowfall. Most bears don't carry identification information, so some of them might have been visiting from out of state. More than likely, though, the brunt of the bruins had been Colorado born and bred.

As I walked along the road, I wasn't adding up the unusual statistics for bear encounters. I didn't know that 145 sightings had been reported during a two week period in June, or that a record of these reports is documented by Bear Tracker, a map of sightings maintained by the Durango Herald. You see, I had my own paperwork to contend with.

At a bend in the road I glanced up to check for cars. Stepping out from behind a tree no more than 40 feet away was a black bear, on all fours, and it appeared just as surprised to see me. As it started to stand up, I reached out and took Pam's arm by the elbow and we doe-see-doed in the opposite direction. I could tell by the expression on her face that she'd seen the bear too. We doubled our pace and returned along the road the way we'd come, both of us glancing back over our shoulders, for fear that we were being followed.

Rule number two in bear country: If you see a bear, don't run. We didn't run. We walked extremely fast.

Back at camp, we laughed about our experience, comforting ourselves by suggesting that the bear had probably been more frightened by its encounter with bi-peds. When I suggested a return trip to the outhouse, Pam recommended taking the truck.

"I ain't afraid of no bears," I declared.

"I know," she replied, "but with our luck that bear is the one that uses an outhouse instead of the woods."

CHAPTER FIFTY-EIGHT

Top of the morning

Along Highway 145, eighty-five miles north of Cortez and opposite a set of pit stop restrooms, a lush mountain meadow stretches itself like an invitation to relax. It's called Lizard Head Pass, a summit 10,000 feet above sea level. Psychologists claim the color green reduces stress, and I'm sure there's an inkblot in some psychiatrist's desk that, when scrutinized, resembles a lizard's head. I shouldn't be revealing this, but at this location I've always found a camping place and aside from my fair share of road taxes it hasn't not cost me an additional dime. Occupancy is limited to 7 days in a 30 day period, which is only fair. After all, if the earth was created in 7 days, it shouldn't take more time to recharge a human soul.

This year after dumping my gear for few days on the cosmic couch, I decided on a drive into Telluride. I didn't realize it was bluegrass weekend, but festively colored signs directed any driver that could read to designated locations for "Festival Parking." For the past 30 years live music enthusiasts have flocked to the mountains. In 1974, a mere 500 people settled in to listen. Last year the event attracted 11,000 foot stomping fans.

As I approached the town along the gauntlet (the only paved road in or out of Telluride) orange cones obstructed my way and slowed me to a stop. A young woman in an orange vest waved my car forward and walked over to the window. I rolled the window down and offered her a friendly smile.

"How are you?" I asked.

"Are you going to the festival?"

I didn't know there was a festival, I wanted to say, but I could tell she was interested in the answer to only one question. I opted for honesty.

"No," I said, "I'm just stopping by the free box to hunt for recyclable treasure." Then it was her turn to smile, but I think hers got prompted by a sneaking suspicion that she might be dealing with a wise guy in the middle of a busy afternoon.

"15 minutes is all I need, really!"

I'm not sure if she ever believed me, but she scribbled on a green slip of paper and handed it to me.

"I'll give you an hour," she said rather pleasantly. "But display the permit so it will be visible through the windshield, otherwise you'll be towed."

I thanked her and pulled away from the checkpoint, her warning sounding more like the thunder of an approaching human avalanche. I only had one hour, but I was high with the power of driving into town, the freedom to park anywhere I could find a spot without being hassled by the authorities.

A space materialized directly across from the free box, so I pulled in and got out of my truck. I rummaged through a few shelves, but it was easy to see not much was left to be recycled. I wanted to blame all the bluegrass fans, but a clearly posted notice informed me that the shelves are emptied every Thursday by the City of Telluride in an attempt to keep things clean. Bad timing, I thought, as I hopped back into the car and headed out of town.

I'd stayed for less than 15 minutes and as I passed by the checkpoint I waved to the same woman who didn't notice me go by. Truth be told, my timing was excellent: A Colorado State record for the fastest trip in and out of Telluride during a Bluegrass Festival, my parking permit a coveted souvenir. I'd have had it autographed by a celebrity, but I'd not been in town long enough to study the faces.

As I got to considering my situation on the drive back to camp, I could see the kind of freedom that was important to me: The wind strumming branches through a tangle of needles, the melody of birds at daybreak, snow melt trickling down a keyboard of bright and dark stones as it tumbles into the Dolores valley.

I spent the night in the shadow of the lizard. Though it was the middle of June, it got cold. At daybreak I rose and hiked in the direction of the burgeoning sunrise. One face of Sunshine Mountain was beginning to glow and I knew the world was warming up. You see, it's a different kind of live music that requires an audience of only one, with patience enough to stay from the beginning of one day all the way through the encore.

CHAPTER FIFTY-NINE

John Muir, go home

Any experienced summer traveler might have pointed to my wife and me as classic examples of clueless tourism: See what you get when you travel without an itinerary? When you think camping has something to do with owning a tent? I can hear them stifling their snickers, trying to sound sympathetic but finding no compassion.

We'd pulled into three campgrounds run by the U.S. Forest Service and found no place to stay for the night. Although many sites were still unoccupied, each had a white sticker clipped to its driveway post declaring that plans had officially been made. It was our own fault: we'd left home at the ridiculously late hour of 8 a.m., driven for eight hours through an inspirational landscape where we'd succumbed to the temptation of stopping to look at the scenery. Worst of all, we'd neglected to call ahead with a valid credit card in order to guarantee a camping reservation.

We deserved what we didn't get.

Then we just got lucky. One loop of the Redstone Campground in Colorado's White River National Forest had witnessed a modern day miracle: Rangers received a cancellation – something that hadn't happened in the last six months, according to our campground host. Site number 11 ended up being the one tucked a little too near the privy, but we took it, paid $18 for one night, and joked that a 15' X 15' gravel pad might have what it takes to rock us to sleep.

With my lamp strapped to my head, I read a little from John Muir's diaries while someone's gasoline generator rattled the aspen leaves for nearly an hour. Then I closed my book and listened to the evening serenade of another camper's boombox featuring a country singer whose heartache should have stayed back on the ranch. The burnt umber sunset had long ago vanished behind the horizon, but when the security lights for the toilet came on, I answered the call and did what nature required of me.

I thought about John Muir, who wrote in 1895: "You know that I have not lagged behind in the work of exploring our grand wildernesses, and in calling everybody to come and enjoy the thousand blessings they have to offer." Well, John, they're all here, every one of them from what I can tell, and I think it's about time somebody withdrew your invitation. I guess camping will never again be what it was in your day: A primitive excursion away from the security and sameness of our homes and into the unpredictable unknown.

At the beginning of the 20th century Muir perceived our public lands as places of "spiritual power" where the soul could be recharged by the earth's "divine beauty." Clearly a romantic, John Muir would be discouraged to see how tourism has been exploited for profit by the very agencies charged with protecting it at the beginning of the 21st century.

Of course, times change. Muir's idea that by seeking wilderness people could purge themselves of the "sediments of society" has really lost its appeal. More and more, it seems, campers flock to our national forests carting the trappings of our society with them. Out of 40 reserved sites along the Crystal River, I counted only five that contained tents. The rest were what I call "wireless homes." They function just like the places left behind, but from a more remote location.

The big rigs sometimes haul cars and pull in with ovens, refrigerators, satellite TVs, stereos, showers, hot water heaters, air conditioners, and furnaces.

Though the human spirit will always seek some connection to the natural world, I think the human brain has trouble getting past its busy signal. Muir believed that "thousands of tired, nerve-shaken, over-civilized people are beginning to find out that going to the mountains is going home." Thanks to our federal agencies that manage the outdoors for us, we have built way stations in the woods that translate Muir's belief just a little too literally.

Eventually, the posted rules for our campground's curfew took effect and things quieted down. I got up to stroll around our loop and saw more than a dozen fire rings kindled on this warm summer night. At first, I was struck by the absurdity of the scene, because the last thing anyone needed was a crackling fire. But when I wandered even farther away from the society of campers, out of the loop and along a path through the moonlit trees, I glanced up at the sky and noticed there, too, all those stars, still burning.

section seven

The Road, Again

CHAPTER SIXTY

A wing and a prayer

A small, red Ford Fiesta would not be considered a luxury car, but the trip to Arizona felt luxurious. We had – or rather, the couple that took this trip had – an entire week. I'm not going to identify that couple, because the police might take more than a reader's interest in the story I'm about to relate. But it happened almost exactly the way I remember it, or rather, the way I remember it being told.

Queen Valley is located on the edge of the greater Phoenix sprawl, and a few retired folk summering in the Four Corners area actually own wintering property near Phoenix. The car in question did not belong to the drivers. You see, the young and generous couple I referred to had offered to pick up a few things from the older couple's hibernating home while on the road and heading in that general direction. So, the car belonged to the older couple, who had it gassed up before loaning it to the younger ones – a petroleum based thank you for the kind offer. Some kindnesses can never be repaid, as you will see, and should therefore never be offered.

Near the Four Corners Monument the more curious of the two young people peeked into the glove compartment.

"You never know," she said as she pushed the button, "what might be required in an emergency."

Certainly, a medium caliber handgun was not the kind of emergency tool this passenger had in mind. In fact, the discovery of the handgun felt like an emergency in itself.

"Don't touch it!" the driver exclaimed. And she didn't, so she closed the tiny glove compartment door and they pretended what they'd seen wasn't there, but already it was holstered in their imaginations, and loaded.

I can't imagine why an older couple would have left a handgun in a car they loaned out to other people. Or at least that's what the driver probably thought. Maybe retired military men don't concern themselves with how things appear in a demilitarized world.

The trip would have been uneventful after finding the handgun except that it wasn't. Flat on the road, halfway across the Checkerboard reservation, a giant bird of prey had come to its end, a traffic fatality with feathers. They stopped.

"Wow," he remarked. You see, he was still driving, and drivers are allowed to stop beside anything that elicits a capital Wow. He identified the bird as an eagle, a dead one. It had been crushed by more than one vehicle. While dragging its enormous carcass to the side of the road an unfortunate idea occurred to the driver: Tucson LoneEagle would appreciate the gift of these feathers. And so, with the grace of a trash collector, he separated the best wing from the carcass and flung it under the lid of what served as a trunk in a vehicle that size, covered it with a tarp, and continued down the road. I know this for a fact, that they were feeling guilty about breaking several laws: One against the transport of dead eagle parts, and the other about possessing weapons that could not be accounted for by registration or permit. One of them thought (I can't remember which), At least we aren't smuggling drugs.

But drugs would have been small stuff compared to the reason the two police cars converged on the tiny red Fiesta with sirens and lights. Oh shit! One of them thought. I'm pretty sure this time it was the driver, not the passenger who unconsciously pressed her knees against the glove compartment door.

Two Arizona State patrolmen, guns drawn, asked them to get out of the vehicle. After identification had been provided, the patrolman that stood guarding the suspects visibly relaxed; his handgun pointed toward the pavement. When his partner signaled from the patrol car, the gun went back into its holster.

He apologized for the excitement and informed the couple that a car identical to the one they were driving had been involved in an armed bank holdup. The criminals were supposedly in flight at this moment. The officer's use of the words, "in flight" had not been intended to make anyone nervous, but the young driver visibly flinched as the words hovered in the air.

One of the police radios crackled to life and the patrolman rushed back to his own car. In the time it takes for thunder to boom after a lightning strike, the two patrol cars sped off in opposite directions.

I don't know if relief can be said to fall like rain on a desert, but the sky surrounding the couple left standing beside their borrowed car literally went soft. Maybe it was the driver's knees, I'm not sure. Like I said, I only heard the story, third hand really, and the details will always be suspect.

CHAPTER SIXTY-ONE

Praise the Lord and pass the pancakes

Drive across the West along an interstate and you'll get the impression that sleeping, eating, and getting gas are the activities we hold dear to our hearts. I'm not saying they're not, but of these three, the greatest seems to be eating.

I'd stayed overnight at a motel no driver could see, much less imagine, just off the Interstate. It probably had been built in the 1920s, remuddled in the 1950s, and then pretty much left as a landmark to ineptitude for the last 50 years. No HBO, no ice machine, no continental breakfast, no security device unless a doormat that wouldn't lie flat had been intended to trip intruders as they skulked past my door. My room had no fewer than three double beds. A young clerk bottle-feeding her infant checked me in. She gave me the single rate and expressed relief that I'd taken the last room, for then she could flip the switch and put power to the word "No" on the neon "Vacancy" sign above the door; we could all rest assured: The motel was full.

The next morning I drove back toward the Interstate for breakfast. The Golden Trough sported a towering sign visible at least a half mile away. I pulled into the parking lot, locked up, then patiently stood beside the plaque just inside the door that announced, "Please Wait to be Seated."

"Table for one?" the hostess inquired.

"Yes, please."

"Did you get a ticket?" she asked.

"No, I carefully observed the parking lot speed limit when I pulled in."

Her body language smirked, Another guy who thinks he's funny, but all she said was, "I mean, for the breakfast buffet. You'll have to wait a minute."

Three other breakfast parties had crowded in behind me and she glanced toward them with a rekindled graciousness. "Tickets?" The party directly behind me waved their stubs in the air, as if they were bidding on the prize sow at a livestock auction.

Before the words "If you'll come this way" could be uttered, the entire clutch of tourists pushed past me, making a beeline toward the seating area.

I had unknowingly stepped into one of the many (but often not talked about) Buffet Triangles. Unlike its namesake, the Bermuda Triangle, people crossing into this vortex don't disappear – they just get substantially larger. It's the hundreds of pounds of meat, potatoes, eggs, and pastries that simply vanish. Just like that. Had I chosen to spend the night at a major motel along the Interstate I'd possess my own ticket, a complimentary breakfast coupon packaged with each room's rental. Instead, I ended up at the Goldilocks Inn, where I got three beds and none of them just right. You see, last night I didn't feel like patronizing corporate America, the old ball and chain, and this morning the breakfast buffet still appeared larger than my appetite.

The hostess returned like a sheepdog, prepared to herd another ticketed clutch of grazers into the dining room. She glanced at me, remembering that I'd asked for something unusual. I decided to help her out. "I'd like to see a menu, if you have one."

She looked at me more closely, as if a dollop of gravy had stuck to my nose. "You're not ordering the buffet?"

"No, ala carte all the way." I must have sounded French. She gave me one of those looks reserved for wolves, a sideways kind of facial snarl that amounted to a warning not to mess with her lambs.

"I'll have to clean a table. It will be a few minutes." Then she looked over my shoulder. "Tickets?" Another group of hungry motorists accelerated past me toward the dining area.

All three groups waiting behind me had been seated before I finally got ushered to my own table. I ordered a simple cheese omelet, and then sat back to observe the buffet crowd.

There's always a kind of excitement in the air when food is present, an aroma that triggers memories and abducts the rational mind. A buffet is designed to peak the appetite, which is why so many plates carried past my table were heaped like little mountains. A buffet seems to taunt us: I dare you to eat more than you paid for.

Now that Medicare has declared obesity a disease, we probably need to rethink the buffet mentality. The Pillsbury Dough Boy has been America's roll model long enough. I mean, even bartenders can be held responsible for serving drinks to obviously intoxicated patrons. By my count over half the customers shuffling past me appeared corpulent, paunchy, potbellied, or just plain fat. There should have been a designated eater standing by in the lobby.

I'm lucky I wasn't in a hurry, because during the long wait for my omelet, I almost caved in and switched to the buffet. A waistline is a terrible thing to watch.

CHAPTER SIXTY-TWO

Off the road again

Jack Kerouac wrote his entire novel "On the Road" in just three weeks. He used a continuous roll of teletype paper, as if pausing to put in a new sheet of paper would have caused a pile-up on his imagination's highway. Lawrence Ferlinghetti said that Kerouac provided us with "a vision of America seen from a speeding car."

When Kerouac's novel first appeared in 1957, I was just a tyke on a trike. The only 'beats' I knew about were – vegetables?

Now that I'm down the road, so to speak – a retired schoolteacher living without a lesson plan – I realize Kerouac's vision of living fast and dying young is not my choice, and certainly not the road I want to see carved by our energy specialists through our public lands in the West. Perhaps it's time for a new novel.

If Kerouac's highway survives, we'll need some sort of measuring stick to judge how far we've strayed from America's true freedom. Not that romantic, century-old affair with the open road, but our commitment to open land that breathes oxygen into our lives.

My novel will be titled "Off the Road." My main character's quest will take him on a quest, seeking wilderness on the East Coast. He'll get lucky, and a hydrogen-powered runabout will pick him up. He'll take this free ride all the way to Missouri, and then find a mass transportation connection to complete his journey. All the while he'll fiddle with his Golden Age Parks Pass, promising himself that he'll visit every remaining piece of public land on his way back West – on his way back home. The complication in the novel, of course, will be in getting him to these destinations, having lost both his wheels and his wiles, with a snowstorm gathering on the horizon.

But that's where I always run out of literary gas. Surely, the disenfranchised, the down and out, the beat, will always be with us, reconstituted along the lines of Kerouac's generation of beatniks. My generation will likely end up chronicled as a culture of debtniks, of maxed-out credit card consumers foreclosed out of their homes, living with their mothers in their childhood homes – just like Kerouac.

Still, I'd start my novel with hope, by preaching the sermon of the wilderness, a beatific vision of our heritage still vibrant in a futuristic world. Public lands are the closest companions we have with Kerouac's boxcars, beaches and open highways. "Off the Road" will speak for a constituency of backcountry dreamers, disengaged from the current culture's obsession with ATVs, snowmobiles, dirt bikes, rock crawlers and SUVs. It will be a place where the free spirit of America can be passed around like a bottle of cheap wine.

Maybe Willie Nelson will rewrite his song for my novel's debut: "Back off the road again." Maybe in another half-century Americans will become reacquainted with their feet, will choose to walk again, to find a trailhead and celebrate the absence of pavement. Maybe I'll have my character back-packing defunct motel furniture into the parks and lighting campfires fueled by Chinese particle-board night stands. With over half of the world's population already living in cities, see-ing actual starlight might be as mind-blowing as hearing Allen Ginsberg first read his poem "Howl" at the City Lights book store in San Francisco.

Naturally, the natural world will play a big part in my off-the-road version of America. We may be running out of oil, running out of space, running out of money and running out of patience, but if we ever lose our public lands, we will be so much more impoverished, even to the point of having lost our vision.

As for my main character, whatever his name will be, he'll be left with his impossible dream, much like Don Quixote. Every nuclear power plant's cooling tower, coal-fired smoke stack or huge solar-power array and nest of power lines will make him think he's standing beside Yellowstone's Old Faith-ful. Every high-rise will induce him to imagine staring down into an arroyo from the cliff dwellings at Mesa Verde. Every airliner leaving a vapor trail will remind him of condors, glid-ing majestically across the milky white cataracts of his skies.

CHAPTER SIXTY-THREE

Return of the dodo

The Sandhill Crane is a very old bird, some nine million years according to fossils unearthed in Nebraska, but I'm not such a bird brain as to drive to Nebraska in January just to say I'd seen the oldest crane. No, I said to myself, I'm going to impersonate a snowbird and go to southern Arizona, down near Mexico's border, where Sandhill cranes migrate each winter in reported numbers that exceed 20,000, doing whatever cranes do best in that lush mush of grass and soil along the San Pedro River.

That was my plan. Until I spotted the flycatcher.

A Vermillion Flycatcher, to be specific. Actually, I don't know much about bird identification. I stared at the little puff of red through my binoculars, all ruffled against a stiff breeze blowing off the surface of Whitewater Draw. It had rained all night and in the morning the earth was a thick reddish paste that stuck to my boots, increasing my height by at least an inch in my first 100 yards of slogging toward the viewing platform.

I saw plenty of cranes, and they were inspiring. They waded in the water, foraged in the fields, flew in crane-like formation across the horizon. I thought I'd seen it all.

But the flycatcher caught my eye. Compared to a crane, it was a tiny bird, but such an unmistakable bright red against the drab grays and browns of the season. My binoculars brought it close enough to study every detail, from its small bill to its short, stubby tail. I stared and stared until I realized I was looking at something I'd never seen before.

Back at the San Pedro House, a BLM supported birding facility and gift shop, a dry erase board hung outside on the porch with black maker notations under the heading "Recent sightings." I scanned the list: Over fifty birds since the beginning of January, including a Dusky Flycatcher, a Gray Flycatcher, a Hammond's Flycatcher, but no Vermillion Flycatcher. Aha! I thought, so I went inside to let the world know.

A sincere older couple dressed in matching orange fleece vests approached the desk while I browsed through the identification guides on the book shelves. They walked straight to the counter and explained in a kindly manner that they'd spotted a Painted Bunting, which, according to guide books, was not due to arrive in the area until early summer.

"We thought you'd like to know so you could include it on your list outside," the orange bellied man chirped.

"I'm sorry," the person in charge cackled, "that list is for people who know what they're talking about."

I had never seen a Vermillion Flycatcher, much less one in a wild and natural setting, so that tiny bird, though hardly endangered, will always be a rare one for me, but to the bird woman of San Pedro House, birds were a specialized business, which might explain why so many species eventually become extinct. The fascination with seeing something for the first time is woefully underrated. We are only obsessed with seeing it for the last time.

It's also true that too many people have no interest in seeing the world with fresh eyes, which might explain why every mall across America contains nearly the same outlets. If shoppers were the equivalent of bird watchers, their daily sightings list would be the map beside each escalator assuring them that another Starbucks is only five hundred feet from "You are here."

When the couple turned to leave I followed them out the door, keeping my Vermillion Flycatcher to myself. They wandered across the parking lot toward their car, laughing the entire way. I didn't doubt they'd spotted exactly what they described, and judging by their laughter, they recognized the cackle of a Dodo when they'd heard one, too.

CHAPTER SIXTY-FOUR

Fruit flies don't bother me

To escape the holiday snow that usually makes gigantic sugar plums out of the Colorado mountain peaks, we had to drive a long diagonal across Arizona, steer clear of that enormous rut known as the Grand Canyon, and ease ourselves into two reserved lounge chairs beside a resort pool under the twinkling starlight of Palm Springs, California.

Several weeks before we left, packages from friends and relatives containing Christmas gifts started arriving. Among the gifts was a beautifully wrapped fruit box from Harry & David. It showed up the day before we locked up the house. I dutifully tucked it away with our suitcases in the trunk of our car, inhaling its sparkling scent of fresh fruit right through the cardboard.

The temperature was nearly fifty degrees and hardly a snowflake was visible. I can faithfully recall we had forgotten all our responsibilities by the time we gazed at the Superstition Mountains, but that fantasy came to an abrupt end as a warning sign loomed near the California border: Inspection Station – All Vehicles Must Stop!

We straightened our seats, as if preparing to land on an airplane. We didn't carry firearms, or drugs, or deal in the transport of illegal aliens but we glanced at each other, not saying the word "fruit" out loud; still, both of us thinking it so tangibly the image of those plump pears and honey crisp apples hung from our lips.

We'd forgotten that officials in khaki uniforms protect farmers who live in California. They stop any vehicle crossing their sovereign border to question the occupants until they can determine if they are the kind of eco-terrorists who might carry some form of high fiber contraband into an otherwise tan and healthy environment. Believe it or not, we were the kind of people they were looking for.

The pickup truck in front of us idled for a long moment while I watched its driver duck from view, then reappear, handing one officer a clear plastic bag containing three plump grapefruit. The officer's hand remained extended and a single bright red apple got positioned very prettily in the center of his upturned palm. Then the officer's partner motioned the driver through the gate and the truck accelerated away into the California sun.

I pulled up to the interrogation position and rolled down the window.

"Where are you coming from?" the officer inquired.

"Colorado," I replied, with an even voice, smiling a big smile, as if I had just stepped off a ski slope, my teeth glistening like ice.

Then he asked the question I knew he would ask, the one he had been trained to ask, the question he probably mumbled in his sleep for over twenty years.

"Do you have any fruit?"

Now, I confess I hadn't forgotten our fruit: Four tender, sweet, potentially delicious pieces of perfect California fruit that had been shipped to us from California no more than a week before this awkward moment. The fruit had been left by a deliveryman who also wore a khaki uniform. I knew instinctively that I couldn't explain the harmless business of fruit transportation to this officer who was in charge of detaining fruit at the California border check station. His job was simple: Confiscate the fruit, destroy it, and don't listen to excuses. He looked serious. He looked bored. He looked pale, as if he hadn't been eating enough fruit.

"I've got an unopened bottle of wine in the trunk," I offered.

He motioned with his wrist – a kind of get-out-of-here gesture – just as his Nazi-fruit partner mouthed the question, "Should we trunk them?" I stepped on the gas, not even checking my rearview mirror, afraid I would instantly hear sirens and gunfire. I drove like a Californian, my mouth dry as tissue paper, my fingers white against the steering wheel. I drove. When I finally regained my composure, my wife was rapidly tapping my shoulder, motioning for me to pull off at a gas station. I parked the car and turned off the motor. I sat quietly, listening to my heart ticking.

"You look like you could use a snack," my wife offered.

She got out of the car and walked around to the back. "Pop the trunk lid," she shouted. I hesitantly reached down and pulled the latch. I watched the trunk lid rise, obstructing my view through the rearview mirror. After slamming the trunk, she climbed back into her seat, holding all four pieces of fruit. She handed me a pear and an apple, then we sat like Adam and Eve, saying nothing, savoring that forbidden moment.

CHAPTER SIXTY-FIVE

Bloom or bust

Every spring I look forward to one great depression. It works out to be my lowest point of the year, 282 feet below sea level to be exact, a geographic record for the western hemisphere. Contrary to what psychologists might think, I'm always elated.

Death Valley is definitely a hot spot, but not one that qualifies as a spring break vacation destination, which is why my wife and I have made an annual pilgrimage to Death Valley for the past decade. I suspect its very name dissuades most of the spring enthusiasts from coming, and that's okay with us. We covet the emptiness, the openness, that enormous dip in the road that has for over a hundred years embodied the idea of desolation.

This spring, however, we read a news story that promised a different Death Valley. Massive precipitation levels in

Southern Nevada and Southern California prompted naturalists to predict a spectacular wildflower display, a profusion that predates weather service record keeping. By massive, of course, I still mean minimal, but when compared to Death Valley's usual two annual inches, six inches sounded excessive. I prefer to travel light, especially where temperatures can scorch the provisions off your back, so I was packed, ready, and waiting with heavenly patience while Pam hunted through the closet for her digital camera, just in case a few blossoms were left by the time we arrived.

Our preferred route to Death Valley is probably more picturesque than the one the pioneers got stuck with. We usually skip across the Checkerboard Reservation to Flagstaff where a spring snowstorm hits us with the very weather we're trying to avoid. Big, wet snowflakes plaster the windshield and I think fondly about the warm clothing I foolishly left at home. Often I'm wearing shorts at the time, but we crank up the heater and climb higher, toward the Arizona Divide, where our descent toward Kingman unravels, across the Hoover Dam, through Las Vegas, and out toward the rim of our Deathly destination.

I better slow down a minute, because nobody really goes through Las Vegas without having something to say. I just wanted to mention how the water level has noticeably improved in the greater Las Vegas area, too. I'm referring, of course, to the mass of human bodies, which according to scientists is over 90% water. Tourists make up a tide of human flesh, streaming along the sidewalks and spilling over into the streets. I am confident that when Las Vegas figures out how to extract the water weight from a population that won't stay away, the palm trees will sprout for generations to come.

But back on the road. We left the city behind us and headed north, Highway 95, planning to exit at Lathrop Wells for Death Valley Junction. Unfortunately, the road was closed. Flood damage? I thought the notice was a joke.

We continued to Beatty, took a hard left onto a rugged pavement, and crossed into California where the trademark Death Valley experience begins. At the top of a rise, like at the crown of a roller coaster's crescendo, we paused for a long moment to stare down into the valley of Death. The wind was chilly. The floor of the valley appeared white, as if it was covered with snow, but I knew it was alkali. We opened the windows, unzipped up our jackets, and let her roll.

I've never seen so many visitors at this national park, people scurrying across the road, every third vehicle pulled off to the shoulder, photographers pointing cameras, propping tripods, standing waist high in the wonder of a vast wasteland, trying for one perfect photographic image of hope. And Death Valley is not famous for hope. Locations like Furnace Creek, Badwater, Charcoal Kilns, Salt Creek, Devils Golf Course, and Dantes View all testify to a history of hardship and heat.

And I would be a lying sack of Borax if I told you I remembered any spring in the last ten years when the landscape unfolding before us held such an abundance of color. Desert gold, the tiny blossoms that resemble miniature sunflowers, spread itself like a layer of butter at the bottom of a brown pottery bowl. I was looking at the world through beer-colored glasses. Purples and whites complemented the scene. It was magnificent.

I should have been disappointed to find so many people flitting like honey bees from blossom to blossom, but I marveled at the sight. I should have been miffed that my privacy had been spoiled by hundreds of wildflower enthusiasts, but I was renewed to see so many people finding pleasure in such a simple thing as spring. Pam clicked my picture. Luckily she brought her camera, because I would have been depressed without an image to remember this moment by. I guess pixels and angels fit neatly on the head of a pin.

CHAPTER SIXTY-SIX

The irrational forest

I suspect that folklore has always contributed something dark and evil to the primeval forest, which partly explains why early Americans logged our trees so quickly and carted them away. With a steady diet of stories like Hansel and Gretel or Little Red Riding Hood, our lumber babies grew up to be barons who could not sleep properly until every patch of wilderness had been laid flat.

I suspect, too, that children who have not been rocked to sleep in the deep cradle of our national forests grow up with an irrational sense of what living on this planet means. They confuse recreation with creation, believing that wilderness access has something to do with improving our public lands. They forget that our first churches were cathedrals of living limbs buttressing a blue sky. They even think the word green is a political statement, not a color by which we judge the vitality of the earth's lungs.

285

I had the chance to drive through the Olympic National Rain Forest. I'd never been in a rain forest. The weather cooperated nicely, because it rained hard, a torrent of water during the entire trip, which explained so much better than words why the area is called a rain forest. My destination was Port Angeles, Washington, but I drove a hundred miles out of my way just to satisfy my obsession for trees. I wanted to be immersed in them like a fish is immersed in the ocean.

Of course, spring on the Northwest coast means rain. For those who prefer a more traditional season, there are mountains in the cold distance like Mount Rainer where skiers gather, but snow has never been an attraction for me. After all, I was born and raised in a place my brother still refers to as Minnesnowta. I prefer the temperate seasons, the slow green growth of timber, the tall limbed reach of lumber. Ski resorts make money cultivating snow, an entirely renewable resource if there is no drought, and while I'm certainly not against using our forests as resources for growth, I'm soundly opposed to growth that outdistances our resources.

At Port Angeles, the trees gave way to an ocean of water and a tide of travelers disembarking or boarding the ferry that shuttles between the States and Canada's Vancouver Island. My plans included a visit to The Butchart Gardens – 55 acres of premier floral show gardens, cultivated on the site of a turn-of-the-century cement limestone quarry. There's a Rose garden, a Japanese garden, a Sunken Garden, a Piazza, a Star Pond, an Italian Garden, and a Mediterranean Garden. There is no rain forest.

I walked for over four hours through these gardens, impressed by them all. Unfortunately, I forgot my camera. I realize how stupid it seems to visit one of the most famous floral gardens in the world without a camera, but the few images I retain exist because they entered through the lens on my cornea and have been archived in my brain. If I scratch my head with my finger to remember a particular garden arrangement, then I pretend the memory is digital.

But the memory of the rain forest has stayed rooted inside me, just like my childhood. No camera lens could have captured it. Oddly, I had my camera with me at the time I passed through the rain forest, but even then I realized the futility of harvesting such a place with mere pixels.

Each time I drive past a sign designating the boundary of a national forest, I feel a tiny pang of trepidation. As a young Boy Scout I once misread such a sign, thinking it announced the entrance to an irrational instead of a national forest. I asked my scoutmaster who was driving the van if we were crazy to be going in there. He glanced toward me with a puzzled expression.

"When you grow up," he said, "you'll understand we'd be crazy if we didn't."

Chapter Sixty-seven

Used karma

Most people who believe in karma know that, like starlight, it often takes more than a lifetime to reach the individual who deserves it. Karma, for those of you who skipped the '60s, is that quirky mystical approach to justice that occurs without the intervention of the police department or a lengthy court proceeding. Karma could save taxpayers lots of money if the cosmos served up humanity's just desserts a little more like fast food.

My wife and I witnessed a perfect example of karma as we headed back to Cortez along a stretch of highway between Canon City and Salida. Later, we decided that we may have inadvertently upset some kind of natural balance that is necessary for karmic harmony.

We finished our visit to Denver tangled in traffic, filling our idle time with jokes about good karma and my old

Karman Ghia. Eventually we escaped the city and, as I negotiated the more picturesque Arkansas River curves, a pickup truck suddenly pulled out in front of us. I remember pumping the brakes hard, controlling my temper and managing to say something neutral like, "Well, well, at least we're moving slowly enough to enjoy the scenery."

"But look," Pam said, pointing toward an object as it slipped off the back of the accelerating pickup. "That must be the fastest karma I've ever seen."

I pulled to the shoulder, then backed up to the spot where the object came to rest. I opened my door and picked it up: Just a wristwatch, and a cheap one at that.

Now let me get this part straight, because I don't want to get sued: The real Nick Nolte may know nothing about what happened next.

We saw the same truck parked on the shoulder not more than a mile upriver. A man in bare feet was hobbling across the gravel, as if the earth was a bed of hot coals. He must have been searching for a better fishing hole and this new spot meant another chance for him – a place to redeem himself in the river of time, to improve his judgment, to cast for better things. (Remember, I'm just speculating here).

I pulled over once more and Pam rolled the window down.

"Excuse me," she called. The man limped closer to our car.

"This wristwatch fell off your truck back there when you pulled out."

The man gave us a huge Hollywood grin, teeth shining like the lights of a boulevard marquee. I swear, he looked just like Nick Nolte, but I didn't say anything, sympathetic to the possibility that some people are obliged to spend their lives looking like somebody else.

"Well, I'll be," he replied. "I keep losing these watches. That's about the 15th one I've bought."

We both giggled appreciatively, sensing this was a moment. We stared at him. He stared at his watch. Then he leaned closer to the open window and looked into the car.

"I'll remember you two," he crooned, as if delivering an Academy Award performance.

He was good. And we believed him in that flicker of sunlight beside a backdrop of the Arkansas River, because everything about this encounter was unreal. Movie stars are encouraged to tell lies without ever being held accountable.

Don't get me wrong: We didn't mind being lied to by Nick Nolte. In fact, we laughed about it all the way to Cortez.

When we stopped for gas and told an attendant of the incident, he informed us that Nolte actually did own a ranch somewhere in the vicinity.

I still don't know if we actually returned Nick Nolte's wristwatch, but it doesn't matter. I just hope whoever he was doesn't get the idea that driving like he did will always be rewarded.

CHAPTER SIXTY-EIGHT

Into a whiteout

Sometimes it can't be helped, that long drive across the wide open, rolling the odometer like a slot machine that promises to pay off with just one more spin. The gas gauge hovers around "half" and it looks like you'll get there without stopping again in the middle of who-knows-where. Home is all you think of, the familiar walls, the mattress that remembers the curve of your hip.

So you settle in, determined to take it fast. The sign at the side of the road says 60 miles to home and you think, glancing at the speedometer, at 60 mph it's just an hour before you get there, the place where you belong.

Though the weather report promised snow before the end of the day, the road has been easy, the sky, a little soft but certainly tolerable. Nothing left but to turn off the cruise control and find a new line on the speedometer. A few snowflakes begin flickering against the windshield, but you expected that.

And it's simple stuff, 60 miles and 60 minutes. In an hour it will all be over.

Two songs into your favorite album, the snowflakes start to stick. You flip the wipers to "intermittent" and sit up a little. You'll have to adjust. The snow is starting to accumulate like static on a TV screen, but it will pass, you know it, it always does. The next signpost announces 50 miles to where you'll be laying your head on the pillow. You check the speedometer and notice you've been forced to drop down to 50 mph. You think, looking at your wristwatch, so what! In an hour this will be finished. One hour and you'll be warming your insides, not caring what the outside does.

The entire album is finished. Through the windshield, if you let your pupils stay fixed to that point where the flakes converge, it's a little like being hypnotized. Time itself appears to gather at the vortex of your vision. The whole sky seems to spin yet you remain motionless. The mile marker you just passed indicates 35 miles and you'll be inside the city limits where the streets are plowed. If you slow down just a little you'll not only be safe, but you'll be home. The speedometer reads 35 mph. Just one thin hour and you'll be there if nothing happens, and what could happen? You've got it under control.

When the snow turns to sleet, driven like rock salt from a shotgun, you're wishing you were stuck behind the semi you recklessly passed 25 miles back. Those taillights burning red like the devil's own eyes would be a welcome sight. Visibility is so poor not even the glow from the town you know must be out there in front of you appears.

It's as if every familiar touchstone has been obliterated, the landscape altered so that it exists in no place but your memory. You roll the window down so you can brush away a chunk of ice that's stuck to the wiper blade. It's impossible to stop the car, because you'll never get moving again; it's that slick. Your fingers are numb from trying to knock the ice loose, so you decide to navigate by watching the side of the road through a rolled down passenger window. The heater fan screams, hot air competing with the rush of cold.

Then a beacon of hope shines against your headlights: A metal sign assures you 10 miles is all that's left. Thank goodness, just 10. Daring the two fates of accident and death, you take your eyes off the road for a frightening moment to see how fast you're traveling. At first it doesn't seem possible, so you check again. It's gotten this bad: 10 mph! Simple math tells you you're still an hour from the safety of your home.

It occurs to you that at this rate you may never reach home. Some archaeologist will find your remains centuries from now after they've been deposited by this circumstantial glacier a few yards from the spot that would have been your doorstep. You will be labeled "chronoman." Crowds of onlookers will file past what they have been told is an elaborate steel coffin, gawking at the strange burial ritual of a vanished civilization. You will be another King Tut, set out for display. Your exhibit will tour the earth, fascinate children's imaginations and inspire commuters as they set out for the stars.

Photo credit: Joel Kunza

About the author

DAVID FEELA, a recently retired teacher, is a poet, free-lance writer, and writing instructor. His work – poetry, fiction, and creative nonfiction – has appeared in hundreds of regional and national publications since 1974, as well as in over a dozen anthologies. Essays have appeared in the *Denver Post* where he was selected to be a "Colorado Voice" and occasionally been printed as a contributor to the syndicated "Writers on the Range" series produced by the *High Country News*. For eleven years he served as a contributing editor and columnist for *Inside/Outside Southwest* and currently writes for the *Four Corners Free Press*. A poetry chapbook, *Thought Experiments* (Maverick Press), won the Southwest Poet Series, and his first full length poetry collection appeared in 2009 under the title, *The Home Atlas*, through WordTech Editions. *How Delicate These Arches* has been falling together for over fifteen years.

Designer

ELLE JAY DESIGN

Lindsay J. Nyquist
www.ellejaydesign.com

books
brochures
business cards
letterhead
newsletters
and just about anything else

Press

RAVEN'S EYE PRESS
Rediscovering the West
www.ravenseyepress.com

The Monkey Wrench Dad: Dispatches
from the Backyard Frontline
by Ken Wright

Livin' the Dream: Testing the
Ragged Edge of Machismo
by B. Frank

Why I'm Against It All
by Ken Wright

Manswarm
and the Killing of Wildlife
by Dave Foreman

Ghost Grizzlies: Does the Great
Bear Still Haunt Colorado?
by David Petersen

Visit www.ravenseyepress.com
for a complete listing of our titles.